MEDICINE MIND
BUDDHA MIND

PLACEBOS, BELIEF AND THE POWER OF YOUR MIND TO VISUALIZE

CHARLENE JONES M.ED/M.A.

HEARTONGUE PRESS

ACKNOWLEDGMENTS

I am grateful to be here, since staying alive through 3 days when I was held hostage when I was 16 did not predict such a positive outcome.

I am grateful to all the scientists who have dedicated their lives to unfolding the mysteries of the three pounds of grey matter we cache in our skulls, our extraordinary brains. I am so grateful to the scientists who study the power and intelligence of our bodies.

I am also deeply grateful for all the Tibetan leaders in meditation who found their way through suffering using the Tantric path of Visualization Meditation coupled with the Whispered Lineage called mantra.

I am grateful to you who have picked up this book, perhaps out of curiosity, maybe from a deep need to search but with a willingness to read how recent Western scientific discoveries support the practices of visualization meditation as a path to improved quality of life.

Disclaimer:

To the Mother and Father of the Fairies
And to the Fairies themselves

INTRODUCTION

For the first time in history the entire Western world has access to powerful meditation techniques developed in Tibet and the far East.

At the same time as His Holiness the Dalai Lama explores Western science, notably Western medicine, and extols its virtues for helping so many people through chemistry, biology, physics, neuroscience and more, Western science begins to understand the dynamism behind belief and visualization meditation. We begin to know that believing in a pill, or surgical procedure or a figure of calm serenity has definite impact on the pill, procedure or visualization's success to uplift or even cure distress from emotional and physical pain.

This book explores the seam between those techniques of visualization and the powers of belief.

For visualization I have chosen Medicine Buddha. Medicine Buddha is one example of the many celestial embodiments held by Tibetans to be vibrant, living, autonomous beings. You may take Medicine Buddha as an embodiment of the human hope for, and faith or belief in, medical cures for all diseases, upsets, traumas and illness. In other words, Medicine Buddha here exemplifies a panacea, humanity's hope for medicine that cures all.

As we shall see, some scientists believe our bodies and brains hold such a wide variety of naturally occuring medicinal hormones and molecules such a plethora of pain-relieving substances as might fill a large pharmacy and well beyond.

Medicine Buddha belongs to the Tibetan Buddhist Vajrayana Tantra panoply of meditation icons. The meaning of tantra is union. With enough meditation practice a sense of union is experienced by the meditator with the visualized figure.

Now Western science offers descriptions of how our brains accommodate to whatever we gaze upon. Neuroscience data outlines how our brains create a feeling of oneness with these figures.

If you find another visualization holds more meaning for you, please try that instead. Try to choose a figure that is greater than human as this will motivate the highest level of response. Mother Mary from the Catholic tradition is one as is Confucius.

In these pages you'll explore details of ritual meditation, why things are done in a certain order and why returning to the same practice in the same place time over time yields the best results.

We also include the latest scientific investigations into the fascinating world of placebos. The startling results lead us to understand the strength of our belief, even belief in gazing at a picture or statue while reciting a mantra or prayer, creates a powerful dynamic in building an uplifted, healthy and vibrant life.

Medicine Mind Buddha Mind does not replace your doctor's advice nor the counsel of any medical or therapeutic person with whom you consult. The purpose of this book is to express how visualization meditations line up with Western neuroscience's latest information about how our brains work and the role belief plays in getting us healthy and keeping us well.

The purpose of this book is not to convert people to Tibetan Vajrayana Buddhism, but to encourage explorations of all manner of health and health-inducing potentials of our human mind.

The purpose of this book is to offer readers an increased understanding of how visualization meditation works according to neuroscience and the study of beliefs and place-bos. The book offers ways that some visualization meditations may improve quality of life, especially where strong belief in the visualization plays a part.

Questions about visualization meditation began for me over four decades ago as I sat in the newly constructed Sakya Temple in Dehra Dun India. About 100 of us had gathered at this temple. We experienced daily meditations under the tutelage of His Holiness Chogyi Rinpoche and his translator His Holiness Sakya Trizen.

My questions about visualization meditation began there but being able to visualize took a few more years. The ability to visualize claimed an interest in me that never left. I always felt just a slight bit better after making the effort to visualize in my meditations and still do. In those days feeling better was as rare as snow in July in my home, Southern Ontario. Not impossible but very close. I suffered from what came to be called PTSD although at the time no name existed for the numbed inability to direct my life that rose every morning and followed me into nightmares when I was able to sleep.

In the years between that time in the temple and where I sit today the mystery of how making images in our minds helps us heal never left me.

My Master's thesis is on how to use such images in teaching reading and writing. Now many schools include visualization in their curriculum to help students learn to read and write and to reduce stress. I know the ability to work with both sides of our brains, the logical and organized left side and the visually gifted right-side results in an enriched life experience.

Placebos, formerly thought of as inert and therefore useless, now describe a way in which our brains work to heal. Belief is the prime ingredient needed to turn on the placebos or as we shall see to turn on the effects of some Pharma drugs. Between placebos and belief we learn how powerful our brains are and that may fuel us toward discovering the healing results of visualization meditation.

CHAPTER 1

*V*isualization Meditation, Placebos, and Belief

We begin with a visualization that will empower you through something you already know how to do: read.

Medicine Buddha Visualization

Start at the bottom of the visualization. A lotus flower (you may think carnation or any multipetaled blossom familiar to you) opens with light blue and pink petals.

Medicine Buddha is seated on a full moon disc. Imagine this as a 3-D sphere with the curving edge just visible from the centre of the petals.

He is seated in Vajra Asana, or Diamond Pose with one foot resting comfortably on the thigh of the opposite leg and the other foot similarly at ease on its opposite thigh. You've seen this posture many times.

Notice his skin is blue. The blue is lapis lazuli shade, so it's darker than the lotus petals.

He holds between the index finger and thumb of his right hand, the stem of an herb.

His other hand gently cups a bowl in his lap, a bowl we are to imagine filled with healing nectar.

He wears the robes of a simple monk. Many of the Tibetan iconography wear fine silks and multiple jewels. Here, Medicine Buddha has no jewels and wears a patched and worn robe of orange and brown.

He has no crown, as is usual with other Tibetan meditation figures. Instead you may imagine eight other Buddhas sitting in order, rising from the crown of his head. Or not! Just focus on the main Medicine Buddha.

And his face shows complete serenity. Serenity like his implies a stability that will not be moved. Now the visualization is complete.

Visualizing while reading is one of the facilities many of us acquire naturally and hardly think about. It is a hallmark in good writing that authors appeal to our inner senses through creating details that bring settings and characters alive. The best writers do that through sensory details, allowing us to live through our inner senses the sights, sounds, textures, tastes and smells that allow the author's world to completely unfold in our imaginations.

You do visualize and you likely have since you learned to read.

This visualization of Medicine Buddha will be repeated later in the book because according to neuroscience "neurons that fire together, wire together." Repetition ensures the ability to visualize with increased clarity.

If you chose to use another figure, feel free to slowly construct their details from bottom to top as indicated here.

Placebos, Meditation and Healing

We live in extraordinary times. A bewildering sea of books, CD's, youtube episodes, documentaries, even feature films describe our growing awareness of...something. Something inside us leads to better—better feelings, better states of mind, better health, better relationships, better finances. All this emphasis on how to live leaves many of us staggering under confusion. Which path leads to the promised land of more serenity, less fatigue, harmonious relationships? Which path will make us feel secure?

Many of us know with increasing certainty that calm serenity supports a healthy life but wonder how to remain calm amid all the upheaval, environmental, political, financial, medical and more taking place constantly, everywhere.

Slowly, advanced knowledge of how our brains work is seeping into the culture. We hear bites of information about our brains and personal attitudes and how these are shaping the experience we are having in life, right now.

We will take a look at placebos and how what we believe contributes to living a healthier, more contented life, or not. We will read about and see a detailed example of Tibetan Buddhist Vajrayana Tantra practice, practices in meditation that rely upon our brain's wizardry in creating imagined forms. We'll look at how belief plays into the success of such imagined forms to help us move toward those promises of increased vitality, increased ease and unhampered present moment focus.

This book examines the power of our beliefs and the role of placebos in comparison with Western medicine's belief in chemicals and pharmaceuticals as healing agents. We will see

3

how visualizing an effect from a pill, tonic or even surgery may impact their efficacy.

Focusing on the Tibetan depiction of Medicine Buddha we'll look at how sustained attention and focus, habits of mind that grow with meditation experience, help create potential healing paths for our physical bodies.

It is not the aim of this book to prescribe anything. Your choice towards physical, mental and emotional well-being depends upon your belief. If you believe in Western medicine (and we will see examples of how some Western medicine *only* works when the taker *believes*) then Western medicine including ceremonies such as surgery, are for you.

The aim of this book is to open ways to empower your belief system as it stands. In this way whatever you choose toward increased physical, mental and emotional well-being promises to return the best to you.

Before we go more deeply into placebos, we need a little bit of neuroscience to help us understand how our brains work.

Neurons that fire together, wire together. Neuron is the name given to the nerves in our brains, estimated to be more than 1 trillion! The mantra, neurons that fire together wire together describes not only the actions of neurons and how they socialize, or gab and get other neurons to gab with them, but create pathways, larger neuronal paths of easy access for whatever holds our attention.

Once stimulated in a certain direction, neurons encourage their neighbours to join in the excitement. Once those neurons join in, more continue. In this way, firing certain neurons repetitiously creates faster and faster 'high-ways' for our thoughts and actions.

Think in terms of a forest. At first the path is covered, shrubs and trees everywhere. In time with repeated walking and removing the excess greenery, we can walk through.

Once this has happened, we may widen the path so carts can travel down, giving us our first taste of horsepower. Eventually with enough repetition the path becomes a road, the road a highway and before we know it, we are zooming along an Autobahn of our own creating.

This is how learning takes place, from the earliest steps of a toddler, to understanding and memorizing an alphabet and on throughout life. Repetition leads to habits.

The actions coming from the highways of neuronal pathways are habits. Habits require effort both to make and to break. Some habits or repetitive rituals flow easily and naturally to enhance our lives. Brushing our teeth daily with our own personal toothbrush helps prevent tooth decay, which can be painful, and oral diseases that take a toll on total wellbeing. Brushing teeth also leaves us prepared to meet others socially with fresh breath.

This example may seem too common to matter, but many cultures even now do not have the social beliefs in place that encourage oral health. In the area formerly known as Tibet for instance, many hold the belief that sharing a toothbrush, one among a family or even with extended family, is acceptable. Although some Tibetan leaders, notably Ayang Rinpoche, make every effort to bring modern Western medical knowledge like brushing teeth regularly to the Tibetan people, it is by no means a habit for all Tibetans yet.

We enact rituals on a regular basis in our daily lives. Those rituals bring us comfort through a sense of security and in this we intuit what scientists have discovered regarding placebos and even some pharma drugs.

Scientists and researchers investigating placebos have learned the more ritualized our attention to the placebos we are taking, the more dramatic their ability to effect positive and measurable change in our brains and our perception of pain or illness.

Rituals and attention to detail create a super force in our brains. This super force empowers visualization as well as placebos. Remember: neurons that fire together, wire together. So, the more neurons you have going toward a ritual the greater the effect.

This may be the intuition behind the timing of rituals paid to each of the figures involved within the Tibetan tradition. In Tibetan culture rituals known as Wongs may last several hours, even several days. Some Crown initiations may take an entire month!

Each detail of every day, or every hour of these elaborate ceremonies involves deepening and improving the intricacies of every step of the sacred empowerment. That's why the word Wong translates as Empowerment: having doused your brain for days and weeks in focused concentration on the meditation practice, your daily meditation opens up much more easily. It is easier to pay attention.

For now, we return to Western science and our exploration of placebos.

CHAPTER 2

$\mathcal{P}$ain Gates, Meditation Mastery, and Cake Box Illusions

V.S. Ramachandran, eminent neuroscientist became an illusionist par excellent by using an ordinary cake box and a mirror to fool the brains of his patients into pain relief (Doidge, 2007, pp. 177-195).

Ramachandran focused his research on phantom limb sufferers, those unfortunates who, having lost a limb through accident or illness, have a brain that keeps signalling pain from the non-existent limb. Before we open up Ramachandran's mystifying pain cure, it helps to understand a bit about pain research.

Many of us have grown up in a world where it has been assumed pain originates in the body which sends a signal to the brain. Ramachandran is among the researchers who turned this understanding upside down. He claims pain is created by the brain and projected onto the body.

Ramachandran's view rises from the work of two other scientists, Ronald Melzack, who studied phantom limbs and pain, and Patrick Wall who studied pain and plasticity. These men developed a theory that "...the pain system is spread throughout the brain and spinal cord, and far from being a passive recipient of pain, the brain always controls the pain signals we feel"(Doidge, 2007, p 190). Their research led Doidge to report, "The brain can also close a gate and block the pain signal by releasing endorphins, the narcotics made by the body to quell pain." (2007, p. 190).

Does meditation lead to an increased ability to close the pain gates?

A story unfolds from the dying process of the beloved 16th Karmapa, head of the Karma Kagyu lineage of Tibetan Buddhism. This lineage is known as the most mystical of the four: Gelug, Kagyu, Sakya and Ningma. The 16th Karmapa is still held in reverence as having been a deeply developed mystic.

Karmapa was in a hospital in Chicago. He was very ill and many of the Rinpoches (teachers of Tibetan Buddhism) had gathered to be near him. His Holiness was under the care of Dr. Mitchell Levy who made the following report:

> At the end, [His Holiness] said to me, "There is one thing that is very important for you to understand. If I am needed here to teach sentient beings, if I still have work to do here, then no disease will ever be able to overcome me. And if I am no longer really required to teach sentient beings, then you can tie me down, and I will not stay on this earth." This was certainly an interesting way to get introduced to one's patient....People there—the hospital staff as well as visitors— were just completely overwhelmed by him. Most of them were Christian, and none of them knew the first thing about Buddhism, but they had no hesitancy whatever in calling him His Holiness. They never once said, 'Karmapa,' it was always 'His Holiness.' The staff couldn't stop talking about his compassion and about how kind he seemed. After four or

five days, the surgeon—a Filipino Christian—kept saying to me, "You know, His Holiness is not an ordinary man. He really doesn't seem like an ordinary person." Just the force of his will and his presence were so powerful, that [everybody was] completely taken with it.

... early on the day he actually died, we saw that his monitor had changed. The electrical impulses through his heart had altered in a way that indicated that it was starting to fail. And so we knew, the surgeons knew, that something was imminent...Then his heart stopped for about ten seconds. We resuscitated him, had a little trouble with his blood pressure, brought it back up, and then he was stable for about twenty-five minutes, thirty minutes, but it looked like he had had a heart attack. Then his blood pressure dropped all the way down. We couldn't get it back up at all with medication. And we kept working, giving him medication, and then his heart stopped again. And so then we had to start pumping his chest and then, at that point, I knew that this was it. Because you could just see his heart dying in front of you on the monitor. But I felt that we needed to demonstrate our thoroughness as much as we could, to reassure the Rinpoches. So I kept the resuscitation going for almost forty-five minutes, much longer than I normally would have. Finally, I gave him two amps of intra-cardiac epinephrine and adrenaline and there was no response. Calcium. No response. So we stopped and this was the point at which we finally gave up. I went outside to make the call to Trungpa Rinpoche to tell him that His Holiness had died. After that, I came back into the room, and people were starting to leave. By this time, His Holiness had been lying there for maybe fifteen minutes, and we started to take out the NG tube, and... all of a sudden I look and his blood pressure is 140 over 80. And my first instinct, I shouted out, "Who's leaning on the pressure monitor?" ... Because I knew that for pressure to go up like that, someone would have to be leaning on it with... well, it wouldn't be possible.

Then a nurse almost literally screamed, "He's got a good pulse! He's got a good pulse!" ... His Holiness' heart rate was 80 and his blood pressure was 140 over 80, and there was this moment in that room where I thought that I was going to pass out. And no one said a word. There was literally a moment of 'This can't be. This can't be.' A lot had happened with His Holiness, but this was clearly the most miraculous thing I had seen... This was not just an extraordinary event. This would have been an hour after his heart had stopped and fifteen minutes after we had stopped doing anything ...

To me, in that room, it had the feeling that His Holiness was coming back to check one more time: could his body support his consciousness?... Just the force of his consciousness coming back started the whole thing up again —I mean, this is just my simple-minded impression, but this is what it actually felt like, in that room.

Shortly after we left the room, the surgeon came out and said, "He's warm. He's warm." And then... the nursing staff was saying, "Is he still warm?" After all that had happened, they just accepted it. As much as all that had happened might have gone against their medical training, their cultural beliefs, and their religious upbringing, by this point they had no trouble just accepting what was actually occurring.

His Holiness remained meditating in his hospital bed for three days, and then moved on to take his rebirth as the Seventeenth Karmapa. It was a mark of His Holiness' wisdom and tremendous kindness toward his Western disciples that he opted to display his death process in a hospital in Chicago, USA. In the case of masters as highly attained as the Karmapa, after their body apparently ceases functioning, there are often external signs indicating that they are still in a meditative state, controlling the transition to their next life. In Tibetan monasteries it is customary to permit people to view such masters as they sit in post-mortem meditation, their bodies still supple and fragrant. Seeing what serious spiritual practice makes possible greatly enhances viewers' faith, and also demystifies the death process. (Kagyu.org/the-16th-karmapa)

The length of this quote demonstrates the importance of more than one truth. One truth we see clearly is that we know so little about our brains and their remarkable capabilities!

Here, a Western doctor completely without training in Tibetan Buddhism recounts how this deeply developed person, His Holiness the 16th Gyalwang Karmapa spoke to his doctor.

A mighty reversal of what we believe is supposed to happen—doctors are supposed to advise patients! Instead of the doctor signalling when death might happen, or offering comforting words, His Holiness made it clear he would leave under certain circumstances and only under those circumstances.

I met His Holiness the 16th Gyalwang Karmapa and had several opportunities to communicate with him. One moment in particular stands out.

We, a small band of members of the Dharma Centre of Canada had worked hard for three months to prepare our centre for this momentous event, the arrival of His Holiness and his retinue of 21 Tibetan dignitaries. We were particularly pleased to have put in plumbing in the building where His Holiness was to stay. It was humble, but clean and now, adequately appointed.

As Chairperson, I was summoned to the cabin soon after His Holiness arrived.

I stood in the frigid early April air as evening dusk fell quickly around us. His Holiness' assistant, Tenzin spoke to me from the other side of the cabin's threshold.

"You must get us a hotel. This circumstance will not do for His Holiness."

I stood amazed. A holy man asking to be treated like a rock star? Surely there was some mistake!

Just then, His Holiness appeared behind the assistant. As I focused on His Holiness a warm stream of golden light flowed from his heart to mine, from my heart to his. This was entirely visible to me and I felt if I reached out I might touch it.

Then Tibetan syllables flew back and forth and the assistant turned back to me.

"His Holiness says it will all be just fine."

Stunned, I turned and left.

When I first learned of his passing, and the miraculous details involved, I had no trouble believing what I heard.

We can theorize. Karmapa as a meditation master had access to the pathways of endorphins. He knew from years of practice how to distract himself away from the physical pain in his body. He knew how to prevent his brain from sending signals of pain and discomfort to his body. And he knew much more.

We have examples in other parts of the world. The ability of our brains to turn down the pain signals is well known among soldiers, who often don't feel pain but keep fighting. Doctors know that a patient who expects to get pain relief from a medicine does even when the medicine is a placebo. More on that later.

For now, focus on this—we feel the degree of pain our brains allow. That means we can choose to turn down the pain signals.

Phantom limb sufferers are in a particular fix. They do

not have the physical limb their brain tells them is still present. And their brain tells them that the non-existent limb is still in pain. How to turn off the gateways to a limb that does not exist?

Ramachandran believes "... pain is an illusion..." created by our brain, which is a "...virtual reality machine..." (Doidge, 2007, p.192).

What Ramachandran did was fight non-existent fire (pain) with a cake box and mirror.

He got an ordinary cake box and down the centre placed a mirror. He then asked the phantom limb sufferer, whose arm had been lost in a motorcycle accident a decade earlier, to put both arms and hands into the box through holes in the box's side. The patient was instructed to sit so he could only see his good arm with that reflection in the mirror. Then the patient moved his good arm any way he wanted for about ten minutes.

The brain of this sufferer 'saw' the mirror image as though it was the phantom limb and since this limb was moving freely without pain, stopped sending pain signals. People with phantom limbs started getting relief from their pain through tricking the brain into believing a mirage was a phantom limb!

Because the brain of the phantom limb sufferers believed the non-existent limb to be free from pain the pain stopped. The pain was stopped by what their brain believed was true: the phantom limb was moving and therefore not in pain.

Belief, and belief at a level few of us understand plays a major role in how we heal, whether our brains know this, or not.

Neurons, the nerves held within our skull, extend in what is estimated to be trillions throughout our physical brains. These nerves and nerve pathways excite with stimulation from the outside world and leap with a tiny electrical charge with each thought.

Some of these neurons are called Mirror Neurons and to a surprisingly large degree mimic whatever holds our attention. Both consciously and unconsciously we grow into becoming whatever our attention brings to us.

This is more than an interesting possibility. As we will see it is taken by our brains as fact—what we focus upon, we become.

Marco Iacoboni, author of *Mirroring People*, states "...solid empirical evidence suggests that our brain are capable of mirroring the deepest aspects of the minds of others—intention is definitely one such aspect—at the fine-grained level of a *single brain cell*." (2008, p. 7). The italics are his.

This business of whether we can know the intentions of someone is to the heart of several experiments conducted by Iacoboni and a team of scientists led by Leo Fogassi. The results demonstrate clearly, "Mirror neurons let us understand the intentions of other people." (2008, p.35).

The same principle holds true to sound. Iacoboni expresses it using the sound of breaking a peanut shell.

> That is, when we perceive the sound of a peanut being broken, we also activate in our brain the motor plan necessary to break the peanut ourselves, as if the only way we can actually recognize that sound is by stimulating or internally imitating in our own brain the action that produces the sound. (2008, p. 36).

This merging of the actions and sounds of another are captured in what Iacoboni states, "...watching somebody else's actions and their consequences should activate the representations of your own actions, which are typically associated with the same consequences." (Doidge, 2008, p. 51).

We can know through Western science's latest research that by contemplating a figure designed to radiate qualities of empathy, compassion and a complete intention to heal, we activate the healing potential in our own being. To use the words of philosopher Merleau-Ponty, "It is as if the other's intention inhabited my own body, and mine his." (Iacoboni, 2008, p. 78).

We have learned that neurons that fire together wire together. We have looked at Medicine Buddha as an example of health and emotional stability. We have seen from Western science that our brains mimic through sight and sound what our attention falls upon.

We have considered pain as a function of our brains, a function capable of being reduced by pain-gates, or in fact by illusions like a cake box and mirror.

Now we turn to what attention means. We turn to what scientists and doctors are discovering about placebos and we'll learn some simple neuroscience to strengthen our belief in the power of visualization meditation, or imagination, to help us heal.

∼

CHAPTER 3

*T*he Power of Attention

Iain McGilchrist states he expected his tome, *The Master and His Emissary* to be read by a few scientists. So far it has been read by over 100,000 people, was long listed for the 2010 Royal Society Prize for Science Books and shortlisted for the 2010 Bristol Festival of Ideas Book Prize.

He states,

> Our attention is responsive to the world. There are certain modes of attention which are naturally called forth by certain kinds of objects. We pay a different sort of attention to a dying man from the sort of attention we'd pay to a sunset, or a carburetor. However, the process is reciprocal. It is not just that what we find determines the nature of the attention we accord it, but that the attention we pay to anything also determines what it is we find...Attention is a moral act; it creates, brings aspects of things into being, but

in doing so makes others recede. What a thing is depends on who is attending to it and in what way. (2010, p. 133).

Consider McGilchrist's words, "The attention we pay to anything also determines what it is we find." If we gaze at a depiction of Medicine Buddha and cynicism fills our minds tearing through with statements like, "What a waste of time! I'd be better off..." our attention is clearly different and will evoke something different than the moments when we look with curiosity. Why is his body blue in colour? What do the patched robes signify?

Finally, if we gaze with belief that just looking at Medicine Buddha, just hearing the mantra will lead to increased health we bring into focus a very different finding in our meditation. Understand, all of these experiences, cynicism and curiosity, indifference and deep faith will rise during visualization meditation when the meditations are practiced consistently over a period of time. We do not just sit down and miraculously feel better every time, although sometimes that may happen. And we may not end every meditation session with a strong sense of renewed faith. Instead we will likely stagger and stumble along, some days slogging through the repetitions and other days flying like white clouds on a blue sky. And all of this is meditation. It is meditation because it is increasing your awareness of different states of mind.

What McGilchrist confirms is that by looking repeatedly at the figure of Medicine Buddha or one of your choice, we pay attention to an enhanced replica of human health and healing. We attend to this figure as a source of what is devotedly longed for—health and well-being.

Western science also instructs us on how the figure we gaze upon, and eventually learn to visualize internally, affects our brains such that we merge our identity with that of the chosen figure. We increase our own serenity and emotional stability by gazing at and visualizing a figure such as Medicine Buddha.

McGilchrist explores what it means to offer our attention to an object or a person. He says, "...on looking...we enter into a reciprocal relationship: the seeing and the seen take part in one another's being." (2010, p. 165).

As we mature as meditators, we begin to understand paying attention is the primary foundation of meditation, on the mat or in life. Iain McGilchrist explains,

> Attention...changes who *we* are, we who are doing the attending. Our knowledge of neurobiology (for example of mirror neurons and their function...) and of neuropsychology (for example, from experiments in association priming...) allows that by attending to someone else performing an action, and even by thinking about them doing so—even, in fact, by thinking about certain sorts of people at all— we become objectively, measurably, more *like* them in how we behave, think and feel."(2010, p. 28).

By gazing upon and reciting the mantra of Medicine Buddha we *become* more like Medicine Buddha. And notice what McGilchrist states, "...objectively, measurably..." This is Western neuroscience supporting the power of visualization.

Other explorations in Western science also instruct us on how the figure we gaze upon, and eventually memorize and learn to visualize internally, affects our brains such that we merge our identity with that of the chosen figure. We turn to the neuroscience experiments knowns as "Body Swap Illusion". In these experiments researchers discovered when we dwell visually on the body of another, even if that body is a Barbie Doll or a mannequin 8 feet long, we extend our perceived body boundaries to match theirs! This experience can be so strong that volunteers experience themselves looking at their own body and shaking hands with themselves!

The scientists asked volunteers to lie on a bed with cameras angled toward a bed opposite them. The cameras served as another set of eyes for the volunteers. On the bed opposite lay a Barbie doll. Work on the "Body Swap Illusion" continued until researchers found the whole body might be sensed through another's whole body!

The abstract for an article in the online site PLOS ONE puts it this way,

Here we report a perceptual illusion of body-swapping that addresses directly this issue. Manipulation of the visual perspective, in combination with the receipt of correlated multi sensory information from the body was sufficient to trigger the illusion that another person' body or an artificial body was one's own. This effect was so strong that people could experience being in another person's body when facing their own body and shaking hands with it. Our results are of fundamental importance because they identify the perceptual processes that produce the feeling of ownership of one's body. (Ehrrson, Guterstam, van der Hoort, *Being Barbie: The Size of One's Own Body Determines the Perceived Size of the World*, 2011, https://www.doi-org/10.1371/journal.pone.0020195

Western science reveals our brains are capable of exchanging perception of our own bodies for the experience of being in the body of another. This is the secret brain power used in Tibetan Buddhist Vajrayana Tantra for a couple of thousand years—keeping one's eyes on Medicine

Buddha creates belief the one gazing is the same as the one being gazed upon.

Clearly, seeing Medicine Buddha continually in the external world helps us recreate Medicine Buddha's qualities internally with increasing ease. But what is the result from that? How will this affect your world both inside and out?

For that we turn to the power of belief and our increasing Western scientific understanding of placebos.

CHAPTER 4

*P*lacebos, Pharma Drugs, and Pain

Here we explore whether placebos are the panaceas (healing agents for every condition) some believe, or phantasies that help no one ever.

The truth is placebos place somewhere between these two extremes. They act as a remarkable and side-effect free alternative to some drugs, but are not capable, as far as we know, to substitute at all for others. But first, what is the placebo effect?

The placebo effect involves every drug you have ever taken. It is the gold standard by which pharmaceutical companies determine whether a manufactured drug is effective in treating the targeted illness.

These trial drugs are measured against a placebo, which is a substance known to be inert.

That's right. By measuring a potential drug's activity against a substance known to have no activity, pharmaceutical companies determine what drugs will make it through to your pharmacies' shelves or your doctor's prescription pad.

Inert substances are, by definition, incapable of producing an effect, no matter what. However, this illogic has not stopped the companies that manufacture drugs from spending lots of money and taking lots of time to continually experiment, posing their 'active' drugs against inert substances.

As Wayne B. Jonas cites, in an article in Frontiers of Psychiatry, "...the pharmaceutical industry invests up to two billion dollars and takes 12-15 years to get a new drug on the market." (Jonas, 2019).

Yet whether or not a drug, created at such cost and experimented with over such a long period of time, makes it to you depends on if the drug outperforms a placebo, a substance that does not respond.

Couple this with stats from the United States National Health, Lung and Blood Institute. This institute "...analyzed the benefit of the medications that it funded research on for heart disease over the last 30 years. The result was that these drugs added ~8% over the spontaneous or placebo healing rates for those diseases." (Jonas, 2019, p.3).

In other words, 30 years of research and billions of dollars produced a differential from placebos by less than 8%.

Statins are commonly prescribed to help sufferers of heart disease. This despite what is commonly known according to Jonas,

For every 100 people who take a statin for the primary prevention of heart disease, only two will avoid a heart attack by doing this, 98 will derive no benefit (but we or they have to pay for the drug) and 5-20 will suffer significant side effects (Jonas, 2019, p. 4).

Because so much attention has been paid to the way in which placebos fail, in other words to the apparent success of drugs created by the pharmaceutical industry, it has taken some decades until scientists, researchers, doctors have begun to question what positive use may come from placebos.

Here is a dynamic example taken from the book Cure by Jo Marchant. Marchant discusses a popular surgery for fixing bones that have fractured. It is called Vertebroplasty and has been used widely to relieve back pain. In this surgery cement is injected into a bone to fix its line of break. The surgery has been very successful and helped many feel relief.

One Dr. Kallmes began to recognize some startling things happening. The amount of cement injected didn't seem to matter—patients had pain relief following surgery despite how much or how little cement was injected.

Patients also reported pain relief even when the cement was injected to the wrong place! As Marchant states it, "And Kallmes knew of several cases in which cement was accidentally injected into the wrong part of the spine, and yet the patients still improved." (2016, p.6).

Cement was actually injected into the wrong site, the wrong bone, the wrong place in the spine of pain sufferers, but still they sat up from the operation and walked away pain free!

Stunned by what he was seeing, Dr. Kallmes joined with colleague Dr. Jarvik to conduct studies at 11 different medical centres worldwide. Marchant reports,

Half of them received Vertebroplasty and half received a fake procedure. The patients knew they only had a 50% chance of receiving the cement, but Kallmes went to great lengths to make sure that the sham surgery was as realistic as possible so that the trial participants wouldn't guess which group they were in. Each patient was taken into the operating room, and a short-acting local anesthetic was injected into his or her spine. Only then did the surgeon open an envelope to discover whether the patient would receive the real Vertebroplasty or not. Either way, the operating team acted out the same predetermined script, saying the same words, opening a tube of cement so that its characteristic smell of nail polish remover filled the room and pressing on the patient's back to simulate the placement of the Vertebroplasty needles. The only difference was whether or not the surgeon actually injected the cement...

Despite all of the apparent benefits of Vertebroplasty, there was no significant different between it and the fake operation...Both groups substantially improved...But both Kallmes and Jarvik believe that to produce such a dramatic improvement , there must have been something else going on—something in the patients' minds."

The phenomena in which people seem to recover after they are given a fake treatment is called the placebo effect and it is well-known in medicine. (2016, p. 6-7).

Notice the ritual element taking place in this scientific study. The procedure continued to follow the steps expected by patients, even when the surgeon knew the operation was to be a sham. The surgeon continued with the ritual down to saying the same words and opening a tube so the smell would enter the room. The term 'surgical theatre' was never more real.

All of this ritual detail was enacted with strict attention

just as meditation instructions later in the book detail moment by moment how to set up a place and time, how to beautify your surroundings and how to visualize and recite mantras.

Marchant continues her fascinating examination of the power of our minds, the placebo effect, to create healing in our bodies. That is, she documents measurable results discovered by the most respected researchers, worldwide, on placebos. Western science meets the power of belief, and it is belief that supports our visualizations.

Consider Parkinson's disease. This terrible condition with its increasing loss of nerve and muscle control debilitates 1 in every 500 people in Canada alone.

Marchant reports,

> ...a series of trials carried out by Jon Stoessl, a neurologist at UBC in Canada, showed a strong placebo effect when Parkinson's patients were given fake pills...Using brain scans he showed that after taking a placebo, the participants' brains were flooded with dopamine, just as when they take their real drug. And it wasn't a small effect—dopamine levels tripled, equivalent to a dose of amphetamine in a healthy person— all from simply *thinking* they had taken their medication. (2016 p. 12).

Here's what happened. People suffering from Parkinson's disease took fake pills. Their brains flooded with very measurable, very physically present dopamine. Dopamine is a neurotransmitter. Neurotransmitters like dopamine act to stimulate neurons. Dopamine is the neurotransmitter responsible for the high experienced by many people after exercise. It increases feelings of well-being.

These Parkinson's patients took a fake pill and experienced up to triple the dopamine of a healthy person. This was a physically measurable effect. And this triple acting feel-good, naturally-occurring brain response was triggered because these Parkinson's patients thought they had taken their medication, which they knew did make them feel better.

They felt better because they believed they would. Their expectation that they would feel better, their belief, caused a physical, measurable action in their brains.

The world's foremost expert in placebos, Fabrizio Benedetti has a place that sits in the mountains between Italy and Switzerland— right between, with the living room in Italy and the lab in Switzerland.

Benedetti demonstrated through a process called deep brain stimulation just how powerfully placebos change Parkinson's patients' brains. He did this by careful attention to a single neuron.

We recall Iacoboni's comments about how our brains are capable of "...mirroring the deepest aspects of the minds of others...at the fine-grained level of a *single brain cell*." (2008, p. 7). Here we find another scientist, Benedetti, researching down to a single brain cell the effects of placebos on a Parkinson's patient.

Before the placebo, the patient's brain scans showed up exactly like the brains of Parkinson's patients before they took pharma meds.

On the computer screen the activity of the neuron looks like a shopping bar code, much black and little white. This indicates the excessive firing of the neuron, which combined with other neuronal excessive firings results in the shakes and other symptoms Parkinson's patients must deal with.

After the placebo was administered, the brain scans showed the neuron firing just once, in the same time frame, leaving much white space. The neuron now behaved as it does in healthy individuals and in those who have taken their pharma meds. As Marchant states, "Benedetti had chased a belief right down to an individual cell—demonstrating that in Parkinson's patients, motor neurons fire more slowly after injection of a placebo exactly as they do in response to a real drug." (2016, p. 13).

Marchant continues,

> Between them what Stoessl and Benedetti showed was remarkable. Although placebo effects had been noted in Parkinson's patients, it never occurred to anyone that placebos might actually mimic the biological effect of treatment. But here was proof that patients weren't imagining their response or compensating for their symptoms in some other way. The effect was measurable. Real. And physiologically identical to that of the actual drug. (2016, p. 14).

Consider this. Marchant reports doctors and research scientists are exploring a world of healing in which your brain responds identically, at almost the same measurable quantity, from a placebo as from pharma drugs. Our brains and bodies produce the exact biological response in precisely the right amount to stabilize Parkinson's.

It seems our power to believe and that belief to help heal has been vastly underestimated.

How does the placebo effect work? Some researchers believe it works because of a natural capacity of our brains to produce its own pharmacological responses. This may be the key to learning how to quickly go into meditative states to produce the kinds of pain-relieving hormones and naturally occurring opioids we need, such as His Holiness the 16th Karmapa seemed able to produce.

Jon Levine at the University of California San Francisco wondered if our brains' ability to make endorphins, a class of molecules that act as natural painkillers, might help explain how placebos are also able to relieve pain.

Relieving pain is what some placebos do. Marchant states,

> In trials Benedetti identified more natural brain chemicals that, triggered by our beliefs, can turn our response to pain up or down. He found that when people take placebo painkillers in place of opioid drugs, these don't just relieve pain, they also slow breathing and heart rate, just as opiates do. (2016, p. 17).

Here is another measurable, physical response to taking inert substances, telling us that the power of our minds and beliefs plays a significant, if not a determining role in helping reduce pain.

Many among us still turn to prescription painkillers when in need. And what is more, these chemical drugs with their side effects often only work when subjects know they have taken them. Their help in reducing pain comes from their role as placebos, stimulating our brains into releasing our own natural pain dulling substances!

The expectation of pain relief triggers the needed bio-chemical response from the chemicals.

In this way pharma drugs replicate placebos.

Marchant reports,

> Opioid painkillers are supposed to work by binding to endorphin receptors in the brain. This mechanism isn't affected by whether we know we've taken a particular drug. Benedetti showed that in addition to this mode of action, such drugs also work as placebos—they trigger an expectation that our pain will ease, which in turn causes a release of natural endorphins in the brain. This second pathway does depend on us knowing we have taken a drug

(and having a positive expectation for it.) Incredibly, Benedetti found that some drugs previously thought to be powerful painkillers *only* work in this second way. If you don't know you've taken them, they are useless. (2016, p. 17).

Is this why pain sufferers often complain the drugs they are taking are no good? Is it possible they intuit that the drugs are not doing anything physical, that nothing measurable is taking place? Far from being cranky and dissatisfied as they are often called, these people may be reading their truth from within their own bodies.

Results of some of Benedetti's experiments are telling us that no matter what we take, the placebo effect is in place.

Jo Marchant reports it this way, "As Benedetti's experiment with the open and hidden infusion of painkillers shows, we experience placebo effects every time we receive a drug." (2016, p. 20).

Is this it? Have we reached the apex of medicine where all we need is enough faith, enough belief in our healing agent and voila healing will happen? Not so fast, says the research.

Marchant explains, "For some medications, the effects are almost entirely a result of their chemical components— placebo statins have little if any effect on cholesterol levels, for example. For others, like antidepressants, it's mostly our minds doing the work." (2016, p. 20).

This is an important piece of the puzzle. Many conditions do not respond, as far as we know now, to the placebo effect. Which conditions do respond well?

For those taking antidepressants the placebo effect news may come with welcome relief. The side effects of many antidepressants, including increased suicidal ideation, are eliminated with placebos. But first, a proper diagnosis must take place.

As a therapist I've seen many people who have been

misdiagnosed with depression. Often what they are experiencing is grief or, just as often, exhaustion.

Most of us experience temporary depression at one time or another. This is typified by a lack of vitality, as though someone turned down the enthusiasm meter on your life. Often when in this emotionally dark inner place, people even 'see' the world as dull. Colours are not as bright, touch feels muted and our senses of hearing, taste and smell may be reduced. This is temporary depression and may last a few months, even a year or so. Many cultures including the West through Alchemy, believe these periods to be necessary pre-coursers to growing. In other words, new life within, a renewed sense of yourself in the world is often preceded by a withdrawal from the world.

Sometimes this experience is confused with on-going clinical depression, where you can't get out of bed in the morning, don't want to talk to anyone and neglect daily activities like showering, dressing or eating. This situation needs immediate help and many trained medical professionals offer such help.

Occasionally depression follows a particularly intense period of activity. This is the body's intelligence insisting we slow our pace until we have once again recharged our energies.

Creative depression is known to be a problem for many highly creative people. It often follows release of a book, or showing in a gallery. It is not pathological and must be born with as much endurance as possible. That output of creative energy has left a trough which must be allowed to fill itself again.

Sometimes depression is an accompaniment of grief. These two shadow each other. Grief may come through loss of a job, loss of a relationship, loss of an activity or partner in that activity, in other words any of the loss life brings. Even sudden success may bring a need for a period of grief as we let go of who we were and learn to embrace the new sense of self. Grief includes, of course, the necessary bereavement of losing a special person or pet.

Notice the wording—necessary bereavement. Our culture indicates a few days, a week at most as a signal post that grief must be put away. In truth, grief may take a few years to complete its cycle.

Finally, sometimes depression and dementia appear in similar ways. Discriminating between these two easily takes place with proper medical testing.

The summary here is most of us will experience temporary depression. It is possible we may turn to antidepressants through a time of temporary depression, but those pills come with many side effects.

We are learning about the disadvantages of anti-depressants at exactly the same time as we're learning the value of exercise, balanced diet, and the healing power of getting enough sleep.

Whatever your chosen course of action, whether taking pharma drugs or naturopathic treatments, increase your belief in these healing compounds. Increase your belief by creating ritual and conscious intention as you take them. More on this a bit later.

What do the drug companies, the Big Pharma corporations whose executives rake in millions of dollars every year in bonuses as well as salaries have to say about placebos and about how their own drugs work? In the case of anti-depression drugs, we find Big Pharma and governments have hidden the truth.

Irving Kirsch, a psychologist and associate director of the placebo studies program at Harvard University, has used freedom-of-information legislation to force the US Food and Drug Administration (FDA) to share clinical trial data sent to it by drug companies. This revealed what the companies had been hiding: that in most cases (severely ill patients are an exception) antidepressant drugs such as Prozac have little effect over and above placebo. (2016, p. 19).

This information has been seeping into our culture for several years. We are beginning to recognize that anti=depressants have failed in their original promise. At the same time as we are recognizing the failure of antidepressants, we are finding data, hard scientific proof in measurable, physical quantities, that *believing* a pill, or injection or even surgery will help, determines that it will.

We have looked at the latest research in placebos, the place belief holds in our treatment, which diseases respond well to placebos and which, as far as we now know, do not.

We have learned that placebos are not panaceas, medicine for every ill known to humanity. Instead we are increasingly certain that some forms of human suffering, varying from bone fractures to depression, respond extremely well to placebos.

Now we examine whether conscious intention such as ritual plays a role in determining the success of a placebo. Does the response of an inert substance, a placebo magnify when we turn the power of our conscious intent toward it?

If so, what does this have to do with meditation on Medicine Buddha or other visualizations?

∽

Placebos on Supercharge

. . .

Finally, the response to the question—why all the fuss before we begin to meditate? Why all the details and preparation before meditation and in closing? Why not just plop down somewhere and close our eyes?

We take as our model the way in which researchers have discovered placebos work best—by applying ritual and conscious belief to the actions involved with taking them.

Creating ritual around how and when you take your drugs whether this is prescription or placebo, organic or chemical, works because our expectations of the end of our pain triggers most of our ease. In other words, belief is one strong factor in stimulating our brains to drop organic, natural painkillers and other kinds of healing molecules into our systems. Belief encased in ritual supercharges the effect whether one uses a pharma drug or placebo or as we will see meditation.

As Dr. Kaptchuk, registered Dr. of TCM describes it, his experiments with placebos focus not on the molecules and substances the way Benedetti's do, but on people. Kaptchuk discovered in researching people with arm pain, fake acupuncture works better than fake pills!

Yes, that's right. Not all placebos create the same effect. Certain fake medicines or procedures work better for certain conditions. Fake acupuncture works better for arm pain than fake pills, but fake pills, Kaptchuk found, works better as a sleep aid.

In exploring these differences Marchant lists,

Big pills tend to be more effective than small ones, for example. Two pills at once work better than one pill. A pill with a recognizable name stamped across the front is more effective than one without. Coloured pills tend to work better than white ones...in general, surgery is better than injections, which are better than capsules, which are better than pills. (Marchand, 2016, p. 16).

Might it be that our natural anxiety prior to a surgery provokes a placebo effect of ritual repetition? Even before a common operation, say tonsil removal, it is natural to experience increased tension.

Perhaps a good friend or loving family member helps us remember the operation has been successfully performed many, many times.. They may project into a post-surgery future imagining how much easier and more pleasant life will be once the tonsils are removed.

This is ritual preparation made conscious, to invoke the best of our natural placebos!

Benedetti explains the power of placebos in this way "We are symbolic animals...the psychological component is important everywhere." (Marchand, 2016, p. 16).

Dan Moerman anthropologist from University of Michigan studies herbal remedies used by Native American healers. He went on to study placebos. He believes we might focus differently to understand more about how placebos work,

> Instead of focusing on fake pills, we should be looking at the trappings of medicine that make us expect to feel better— whether it's the white coat, stethoscope and gleaming hospital equipment of a Western physician, or the incense and incantations of a traditional healer. (Marchand, 2016, p. 26).

For a broken arm, nothing works like setting it properly and getting the right exercise afterward. We know penicillin works wonders to prevent and cure infections as do many of the inoculations developed to prevent diseases such as polio or small- pox. If we add to this physical knowledge a compendium of how our brains respond with natural healing elements under certain conditions, we empower our healing ability.

And that empowerment lies in the meaning of the ritual while we use the technique or take the pill whether placebo or chemical. As Dan Moerman relates it, "…the active ingredient is meaning—the meaning that is attached to and surrounds any medical treatment, fake or otherwise." (Marchand, 2016, p. 15).

The vital point about placebos is not the pill or procedure but the meaning each holds.

Some scientists are just beginning to use imagination to infuse their placebos with life just as we do in Tibetan meditation practice.

Dan Moerman himself employs such techniques, "I talk to my pills," he says referring to the pain pills he takes for a sore knee. He describes how he says, 'Hey guys, I know you're doing a terrific job.'" (Marchand, 2016, p. 17). He uses this technique to boost the effect of his painkillers and get the relief he needs from one rather than two pills.

He argues that how we take our medicine may be as important as what they look like, "In other words, don't throw a pill down your throat while you are racing for the bus. Instead, create a ritual around it." (Marchand, 2016, p. 37).

Harold Walach, a psychologist and philosopher of science from Viadrina European University in Frankfurt, Germany encourages such ritual: take the pill or have the procedure at the same time each day he advises with a conscious intent involving prayer or meditation. Meditate on your healing tools!

Irving Kirsch, the same psychologist from University of Hull UK who used freedom of information to force the FDA to share the truth about drug trials, and who worked with Kaptchuk on tests and studies involving the use of placebos on IBS, suggests using visual imagery.

Read this again. A top researcher in the field of placebos suggests we create with our minds an imaginary situation to help promote our inner pharmacy to release its properties. Kirsch instructs Marchant, "To do this be as specific as you can about the effect you would like a particular drug or placebo to have...Imagine the improvement." (Marchand, 2016, p. 38).

This is exactly the advice given by meditation teachers in Vajrayana Tantra tradition, the Tibetan Buddhist lineage of Visualization and Mantra recitation to students—imagine the improvement clearly. As you imagine the figure with increased clarity and detail, as you continue to recite the mantra, you yourself are growing toward clarity and serenity. Western science has now told us how.

Here we see direct meditation instructions—find a compelling figure of greater than human ability and focus! Allow your imagination to create activity with this superior being, activity that lets their healing energy flow into you.

This brings us full circle to how and why visualization works. Your expectation of improved moods during and after meditating on Medicine Buddha will guide the effects of the meditation, including what hormones your brain releases in response to your visualization.

As you focus on these improvements in meditation, you encourage the neurons of improvements to talk with other neurons, and they with others, until it becomes a natural, regularly occurring event for you to be aware of what is good, wholesome and upbeat in your life. With this comes confidence that more changes for the better are on their way.

CHAPTER 5

*M*editation on Medicine Buddha: Visualize as You Read

Once you have chosen your superior figure now is the time to take a close look. For those unfamiliar with Medicine Buddha here is a simple description of what he looks like. Try experimenting with visualizing as you read the following description.

Start with the bottom part of the visualization. A lotus flower (you may think carnation or any multi-petaled flower familiar to you) in light pink and light blue. Allow your mind to dwell for a moment or so on this, and perhaps to experience a bit of curiosity. Why include such a flower, and why is he sitting on it?

Can you sense the perfume from the flower? Does this help open your inner senses?

He's seated on a full moon disc. Imagine this as a 3-D sphere with the curving edge just visible. That curving edge shines with luminosity just as our Moon does.

The full moon in Tibetan symbolism indicates completion of virtues. It means a person or embodiment such as Medicine Buddha with complete integrity. Imagine that! A moral, decent, trustworthy and loving being of complete integrity, one you may trust, fully.

Next he is seated in what is called Vajra asana, or Diamond Pose with one foot resting comfortably on the thigh of the opposite leg and the other foot similarly at ease on its opposite thigh. You've seen this posture many times. The good news is you do not have to try it yourself in order for the meditation to work! Just get the feeling for a moment of the stability this brings to his figure and to your inner visualization of him.

Now, notice his skin is blue. The blue is lapis lazuli shade, so it's darker than the lotus petals and indicates a depth of colour. Western science tells us blue invites our metabolism to slow down and to relax. Deep blue such as this colour encourages even deeper relaxation.

He holds in his right hand, between his index finger and thumb, the stem of a plant. It's called a Myrobalan, but its significance is as a panacea: it contains antidotes to all known and unknown illnesses and sufferings, physical, emotional and mental. Medicine Buddha holds in his hand the cure for every illness.

His other hand cups gently beneath a bowl. The bowl held at just below his navel is filled with healing Nectar. This posture and the bowl itself with the healing Nectar points to what Western science has recently understood—microbiomes rule much of our health.

What are microbiomes? Only about 10% of your cells are human. The rest are bacteria, fungi, archaea, viruses and other microorganisms that with the human cells keep the balance of health in your body. According to Dr. Joe Tata on Integrative Pain Science Institute's website "The microbiome is responsible for aiding in multiple metabolic processes, increasing immunity to a variety of diseases and has a critical impact on the interaction between your organs." Dr. Tata goes on to state, "The gut is the mansion of most of the microbiomes in the body."

The old saying, take care of your bowels and your bowels will take care of you was never more clearly supported. Here in Medicine Buddha's posture and implements we find a picture signal to our conscious and unconscious minds about how vitally important our guts, our intestines are for full health.

He wears the robes of a simple monk. Many of the Tibetan order of celestial beings upon whom we can meditate wear fine silks that flow and roll about their shoulders and bellies. They are usually adorned with exquisite jewels on their necks, wrists and ankles. Each of these details carries significance. Here with Medicine Buddha the significance is the lack of elevated items in preference of simple, everyday patched robes.

The message is that all human bodies have the ability, right now, to release some of the potent antidotes for illnesses. Just as you are you are empowered!

The word often used to describe Medicine Buddha is serene.

And his face shows serenity. Serenity implies a stability that will not be moved. Nothing moves him from his concentrated serenity!

Now you have practiced Medicine Buddha meditation. Remember, if you would like to substitute for another superior figure that brings you a feeling of calm, peacefulness or confidence, take this time to examine the details of your chosen icon.

For now, we return to our exploration of Western science.

CHAPTER 6

Self, Others, and Merging Boundaries to Clear Trauma

We have practiced meditating on a visualization systematically. We have examined the truth about placebos and what powerful tools we have in our imaginations.

Here we take a final look at how meditating on a superior figure proves, according to neuroscience, that we become that which we gaze upon, even to believing that to be within our own skin!

Studies show we easily merge identity with figures, whether they are human or replicas.

> Our experiments reveal that healthy volunteers can indeed experience other people's bodies as well as artificial bodies, as being their own. This effect is so robust that, while experiencing being in another person's body, a participant can face his or her biological body and shake hands with it without breaking the illusion. The existence of this illusion

(and the identification of the factors triggering it) represents a major advance because it informs us about the processes that make us feel that we own our body in its entirety. (Lloyd, December 2, 2008, Live Science, Volume 3. Issue 12. e3832)

If we so easily and so robustly acquire "...experience (of) other people's bodies..." it makes sense that our visual and tactile imaginations providing us with figures of superior human qualities like medicine and serenity also easily and robustly provide their experience to our own.

Now we begin to see how gazing repeatedly at Medicine Buddha begins to rewire our brains. By paying attention to this figure on the outer world and eventually by bringing this figure into our own minds we fulfill what McGilchrist states is the heart of attention, "In looking...we enter into a reciprocal relationship: the seeing and the seen take part in one another's being." (2010, p. 165).

We take part in Medicine Buddha, or Holy Mary or whomever you have chosen as your favourite and in this grow to be more like them. Our brain pathways shift to accommodate the qualities we see in them as their intention.

In the case of Medicine Buddha, we begin to take in his body, his face and his serenity as our own.

While we practice these attitudes, we acquire them for ourselves outside of meditation. How? Neurons that fire together, wire together. This means the more you devote some regular time attending to Medicine Buddha practice, you wire your brain to be him, serenity and all.

We understand how attention, as noted by McGilchrist, is comprised of "...reciprocal relationships: the seeing and the seen take part in one another's being." (2010, p. 165).

Obviously, we believe the picture itself or Tangka of Medicine Buddha does not engage with you in the reciprocal relationship noted by McGilchrist. Or does it?

Have you entered a temple or church, synagogue, mosque or other holy place where devotion and worship have been regularly practiced? Perhaps you have noticed a distinct difference in the peace and calm of this venue compared with what may be bustle and hurry outside?

I lived as a small child only a short walk from a large Catholic Church. Fascinated after finding confetti on the sparkling grey stone steps outside the building, having glimpsed women in fancy hats and dress coats streaming through the doors on Sunday mornings, I longed to go inside.

One day I opened the door. Surprised by the cool darkness, I walked carefully across the short lobby and into the church proper. There I felt something, a calm, a peacefulness that I was to recognize in various places around the world as I grew up and traveled.

Not that all spots advertised as being 'holy' or full of calm and peace deliver such experience, but in places well known as holy sites and in common, out of the way spots, wherever people had gathered over time for prayer, to meditate or self-reflect, the place itself seemed to hum with the serenity those people had invoked. As each person meditated or prayed, using their minds and bodies to create more sanctuary this energy was added to the energy of the space.

And the opposite can happen as well. Where there has been blood spilled, the land itself holds the impression of the tragedy.

My first true experience of this was in a bus tour through Israel. We had been taken to Nazareth, the Jordon River, Bethlehem. We had even experienced the deep viscosity of the Dead Sea by sitting in it.

On this day as the bus stopped, I looked over at the miles of tiny, squat, plaster buildings that clearly had been built for people. No yards, no greenery told of the living presence of these people, only mile after mile of small square buildings, the white light from their plaster bouncing back in the midday sun.

As my feet hit ground a small cloud of dust rose and I registered the endless dust in this place with no trees, no shrubs, nothing growing. A feeling of intense sadness and some other type of despair filled my chest and tears fell.

What is this place? I asked my companions but no one seemed to know. Later that evening I was told it was the Palestinian Refugee Camp.

The feeling I could not identify came from those people who had been displaced from their homes. That was the main cause of all the sadness and sorrow that filled my body. I had taken up the energetic vibrations of this place where terrible things had happened, just as I had recognized the peacefulness of other places.

We leave our strongest emotional impressions in the air around us, and others who walk into the space may notice this. When those powerful emotions are serenity, peacefulness and calm, anyone entering may feel similarly impressed: with calm serenity and peacefulness.

Our activities and especially our emotions in a certain place leave an imprint. Your meditation space in your home, be it a separate room or a tiny corner somewhere, begins with your intention to create sacred space. Ultimately because you bring this intention to every meditation session, it grows into being just that—a sacred space.

You will discover during times of trouble in your life this space, no matter how humble, provides you with a ballast, a place to release, then reset your mind and emotions.

~

More Notes on Sacred Space

I am indebted to Robert Bosnak for the following ideas. During a recent course from the Jung Platform where Robert Bosnak teaches, among other courses, Alchemy, he expressed thoughts on Sacred Space, what it means and how it works especially in relationship to time.

If we consider the usual way we believe in time, we easily see it as a series of events unfolding one after the next after the next. The 'items' in each series may be seen as days separated by nights or sleep. We may imagine this kind of time as a horizontal line rising from a past and running into a future.

This kind of time represents actuality, what occurs in physical space and contains the memories of those events, people and places.

Humans may participate in another kind of time, imagined as a vertical line or axis. This is eternal time, a sense that all is contained in each moment. In this kind of time infinite potential exists. It is possible for anything possible to emerge into actuality.

When you move into your sacred space you are entering sacred time where everything, every potential exists simultaneously. This is ritual time, celebrated throughout the planet by many humans. When you create your sacred space and hold it as sacred, you empower possibilities to exist, even those possibilities you have never thought about.

~

A General Introduction to Meditation

Many people feel confused about what is meditation and what is not. I've overheard people say things like, "Flyfishing is my meditation."

Consider. Two monks stand outside the hut where their teacher waits to speak with each in turn. Each monk is smoking a cigarette.

They go in one by one. The first returns to the spot where he'd met his friend, takes a cigarette out and begins smoking just as the second monk streams out of the teacher's presence and, his eyes widening, proclaims, "The Teacher told me I must not smoke when I meditate!"

"Ah," says the first monk, "He told me I must meditate when I smoke."

Yes, meditation practice will lead to increased calm and a deeper sense of relaxation. Unfortunately, many people in the West have taken this to mean that is the purpose of meditation. They try meditating and when they discover they are more emotional, sensitive or moody, they give it up.

Meditation means without activity. If you discover for yourself that flyfishing or walking in a forest or canoeing in a remote area provide you with a kind of rejuvenation, something you are looking for, then go for that.

When I first learned visualization meditation I heard about something called Awakening. Some people described it as "...a clear sky on a summer afternoon...", or "...a light, like no other you've ever seen..." These kinds of statements rebounded against the cynicism within me. I just wanted a way out of the daily pain of every day and the nightly horrors of nightmares in which I lived.

What no one expressed is that these meditations are designed to raise the corrupt material, the memories of what has hurt you, what has gone wrong, from their crypts. Those memories continue to exercise untold control over your life, until you release their emotional energy. Only then did the feeling of living as though on a summer afternoon rise in me. Calm does come through these meditations, but only after the rough waves have been endured.

So if you want to feel better right now, a little flyfishing or going for a long walk is probably a good bet.

If you want to experience greater stability in dealing with the struggles of life, this form of meditation will take you there.

While calm relaxation provides a definite advantage in almost every way in life, another deeper, more serious and mature purpose exists in applying visualization meditation. That purpose belongs to what His Holiness the Karmapa calls "purifying the Kleshas."

Kleshas are the significant emotional states that act as obstacles to us. Deep unreleased emotional energy is either met with and released through the power of our conscious minds, or it continues to strongly influence our daily conscious lives, and our nightly dreams, to our detriment.

The kleshas mentioned here are summarized in the Yoga Sutras of Patanjali as—Avidya (ignorance), Asmita (egoism), Raga (attachment), Dvesa (aversion or hatred), and Abinivesa (clinging to life and fear of death).

The words of His Holiness the 17th Gyalwang Karmapa may open the topic up more fully. From an article on the online site Nalanda Bodhi on March 6th, 2015 we read:

HH Karmapa focused on the importance of shamatha practice, or calm abiding meditation, as the basis for all Buddhist practice. His Holiness stated that this practice is not necessarily intended to relax the mind or reduce stress but is in fact a practice that eliminates afflictive emotions, or *kleshas*. Reducing and eliminating the kleshas may not be an easy or pleasant task, since this deals with changing our habitual tendencies."

The aim of shamatha practice is not simply to achieve peace of mind and feel comfortable and relaxed in one's mind. Shamatha practice is actually to improve our minds, and to change our personalities for the better by weakening and finally remedying our kleshas. Some people think the point is just to feel good, relaxed and comfortable, but that is not it. The function of shamatha is to serve as a remedy for our kleshas. (His Holiness the 17th Gyalwang Karmapa, *Meditation for the West*, Nalanda Body, March 6th 2015).

While calm relaxation provides a definite advantage in almost every way in life, a deeper, more serious and mature purpose exists in applying visualization meditation. That purpose belongs to what His Holiness the Karmapa calls "purifying the Kleshas."

Shamatha means Tranquility of Mind and the purpose of this meditation is to stabilize your inner state so much that you become resilient. Resilience means it takes a great deal to upset you. Whenever you are upset, resilience means you will return quickly to a feeling of well-being.

Shamatha meditations focus, not on the breath, but on an object, such as a vase of flowers. In Tibetan Buddhist Vajrayana Tantra, the objects focused on are celestial beings. For the most part they are instantly recognizable as human.

The struggle in visualization meditation is to meet the naked mind and feel the power of emotions, without letting those emotions control your behaviour. We learn to sit and let the emotional energy run through our body until it has gone.

Many of us today have experienced badly upset emotions, what we refer to as trauma. We instinctively try to get away from the unpleasant and to return to whatever promises comfort, security and most of all no pain. What we do not understand is the power of those emotions. When pushed below the surface, those emotions continue to tug at us from deep below, convincing us of lies about the world and people in it. Until we experience and release these emotions we are doomed to be under their control.

In this way, our bodies hold the past. Our bodies store the pain of the past. When you receive a shocking blow so big your state of consciousness cannot stay steady in the moment, part of you knows to shut down. For more on this read Bessel van der Kolk's tradition-busting book *The Body Keeps the Score.*

This shutdown is called trauma. And trauma will always be registered in the cells of your body. According to the laws of Chi Gong our cells store the pains of the past by constricting. Blood, oxygen and lymph try to slog through traumatized flesh only to slow down and coagulate. This creates a potential environment for physical illness.

To undo this, it is necessary to release the cellular constriction, allow the emotions stored in the cells to finish their cycle in tears, sweat, howls, sobs or shaking, movements mimicking the initial moments of trauma. Then the body is free of the held emotions.

When the body is freed of held emotions from the past our minds rest easily in the momentary passage of life. Then the exalted states you may have read about in meditation texts, about the cloudless skies and the still waters become states you easily move into.

Perhaps more importantly with repeated practice of visualization meditation, you will feel increased stability, increased capacity to sense well-being, and when emotions do spill over you will find you return to a point of balance much more quickly. That's called resilience.

Not only will you be able to maintain balance in the face of emotional tsunamis from yourself or others, but when you do tumble into emotional behaviour, you'll return to a point of balance much more quickly.

How do I know this? I have lived it.

My early life would have predicted I would be in hospital and under doctor's care for the rest of my life. I was a child of the '50s and as such, beaten. Spare the rod and spoil the child was my mother's only biblical training. My brother raped me and worse, humiliated me whenever he felt impotent. My home was also filled with laughter and picnics, cleanliness and cookies so life was a severe up and down between heaven and hell.

I ran from this home when I was 16 years old and got into a car driven by two armed criminals. What happened as they held me hostage over the next three days was severe enough, I ought not to have escaped.

Having escaped, I should never have been able to achieve a double Masters' degree cum laude, publication of several books, years of performance poetry, career as a professor at a college and then psychotherapist. The chance of a loving relationship with a man I trust felt for a long time like a signal from Mars—interesting but too far away for me to reach. Yet this too has happened.

I am not special or different from you. I was given ways to change my brain and I have practiced this changing ever since. I have held diligently on to the methods of meditation I learned in that temple in Dehra Dun, and practiced in that 3-month silent retreat in New Zealand and many places and times after. I learned to allow the awful feelings to surface, complete with sweat, tears and physical pain. And I have learned that no matter how painful this immediate moment may be while the healing is taking place the rewards exist in having a life that is contented, fulfilled, and peaceful.

If I can heal the pain from such severe trauma, I encourage you to believe, without doubt, you can heal, too.

The world we see is coloured by our semi-conscious or unconscious beliefs. As long as we do not question what we see, the colours of our world remain the same and remain as they first appeared after the trauma.

As soon as we confront the emotions, allowing fear, rage, humiliation and other uncomfortable emotions to rise into consciousness and flood our brains and bodies, we experience relief. The relief comes with a clarity about the world and its life forms, independent of our childhood hurts. Then we are no longer consigned to making the same choice but really enjoy freedom to choose.

A simple example is that well known one about getting bitten by a dog. If you are bitten and no one comes to your aid, no one holds you or worse, the adults around scold you for not obeying or not asking permission, that moment stays frozen within. You may forever hold mistrust about all dogs, or dogs that look like that one. Once the original moment is released, the fear and emotional pain of that moment relinquished into consciousness and the energy allowed to flow to its natural calm, you may make different choices. Your mind will no longer be closed, no longer held to the view that dogs are dangerous.

You get the point.

This simple example contains the same message for all beliefs honed on the anvil of strong and unpleasant, even traumatic experience. Release happens when we face the emotions.

And meditating on a figure such as Medicine Buddha will encourage such release. Repetitive daily meditation over a period of time will acquaint you with memories and struggles you have forgotten. The opportunity exists within this meditation to release the emotions that buried the memories. Once the emotions are released the memories are just that, memories.

In cases of deep trauma, a person's ability to choose a good partner, a safe occupation, a lifestyle that promotes well-being and self-respect is deeply compromised. The result is imbalance: accepting bad behaviour from others, accepting and excusing bad behaviour in ourselves.

In other words, deep unreleased emotional energy is either met with and released through the power of our conscious minds, or it continues to strongly influence our daily conscious lives, and our nightly dreams, to our detriment.

Even without trauma, destructive emotions such as rage, hatred, bitterness, resentment and fear interfere with our daily lives, our sense of how we want to live life. When we are caught in such painful experiences, compelled by these emotions to enact behaviour that leads to more distress, to say words that involve us ever more in conversations and arguments we don't wish to continue, that's when we need the practice of Tibetan Vajrayana, or Visualization Meditation.

When we have practiced Visualization Meditation, we find eventually we are strong enough to stop ourselves from engaging in a reactive response to any outer negativity.

We grow into being stable enough to choose our words, and to choose when to remain silent. This gives us a wider range of spaciousness internally. In other words, we feel calm. This is authentic calm. But it takes practice, and as we will see repetition.

Shamatha Meditation, or meditation on visualizations dredges from the cells of your body those uncomfortable, even some physically painful states you have spent a lifetime trying to avoid.

Neuroscience has established that pain in the brain is not separated into physical or emotional. Pain is pain. Not only are emotional and physical pain zinging along many of the same neural pathways but an emotional pain, such as rejection will affect your ability to think.

According to an article in Forbes magazine "…research from Case Western Reserve University shows…exposure to rejection led participants in a study to have an immediate drop in reasoning by 30% and in IQ by 25%." (Nicole Fisher, *Emotional and Physical Pain are Almost the Same to Your Brain*, February 14, 2020, forbes.com)

Now we know how science supports our visualization meditation practice. We understand visualization meditation leads to releasing emotions and through that providing deeper calm. What is the best way to achieve and sustain a visualization meditation practice?

CHAPTER 7

$\mathcal{S}$imple Steps to a Daily Meditation Practice

According to the Google dictionary ritual means, "a religious or solemn ceremony consisting of a series of actions performed according to a prescribed order."

Ritual may also mean a more secular experience as in "a series of actions or type of behaviour regularly and invariably followed by someone."

You already enact some rituals every day. Your morning may be rituals like cleaning teeth, washing, combing hair. You may have evening rituals concerning making lunches, cleaning up and prepping for tomorrow.

If you work, you undoubtedly have rituals. Driving through traffic, entering your office or home work space, turning on your computer are rituals engaged in every day.

In spite of the rituals we have in our daily lives, we have a cultural reluctance toward ritual. We seem to believe it belongs in the past in churches or temples, mosques or synagogues. It belongs in mysterious societies shrouded and kept secret.

I had a conversation recently with someone who professed interest in meditation, particularly in how I teach it. They asked me about what meditation is, how it works.

I explained that for my students, I start with autogenic training. (Autogenic Training will be explained in the Exercise section in Chapter 8).

I then took this person through a simplified version of what my students experience each week. When we had finished, he remarked on how much better he felt, then asked, what do you do the next time?

It's the same thing. Every week, same thing.

He looked stunned. The same thing?

Same thing is the right answer.

People sometimes come to me who have tried mindfulness training. They often tell me it worked for a while. Many mindfulness training groups sustain for eight weeks. These people who spoke with me found it very difficult to continue their practice after the training ended.

If you end meditation after eight weeks you may have trained some neural pathways to begin to work but sustaining new behaviour in a world that offers you the old patterns over and over is difficult. Although some meditation, some mindfulness meditation training is better than none, continuing a practice is vital to its success in helping you create the changes you want in your life.

It is best to stick with the meditation practice and let yourself simmer in it for at least six months. Then if you do not enjoy it, if you find it of no benefit, if you see no change in your life or behaviour find something else and try it.

When I was a child and wanted to begin some new activity, like swimming lessons or figure skating, my mother would look at me very sternly and say, Yes, you may begin it but remember- once you start you will have to go every week for this year.

This was the 1950's when raising children was a serious event meant to prepare them for a world which had just seen the second of two major wars. My mother's admonitions hold true within reason: give your brain time to really work the new pathways in, to make the transition from tiny sparks of bits of neurons to larger and larger pathways before deciding if meditation, or any other activity, works for you.

It is easier to get into a regular practice through a group either in person or online. Meditation is a process of re-wiring our brains and as neuroscience tells us, 'neurons that fire together, wire together.' The more others participate with us regularly the easier it is to establish the desired behaviour, in this case meditating.

Part of the reason for this mysterious truth is that sitting in a room with other minds meditating allows everyone's mind to get an extra boost. As each participant finds their mind calming and focusing, their neuronal pathways encourage other brains toward the same. We know neurons within each brain light up and excite other neurons. Now we know that each brain lighting up a certain way encourages the next person's brain to light up that way also.

This is what happens in group think. It is extremely bene-ficial for certain activities like beginning meditation. It is also helpful for us to be aware of when we are engaging in group think and to know how and when to step out of it.

First, it is helpful to meditate with others. Eventually you are able to meditate on your own. The path of the individual is a later stage of meditation development.

By the same token, neurons that fire apart wire apart. When we want to diminish behaviours or speech patterns, we will need to "wire apart" the neurons involved until the ease with which we slide into those pathways stops. We learn to neglect those easy pathways for the more difficult choices. For instance, you have always tried to respond with calm caring in all directions. Sometimes what is needed is wrath.

It will take time and meditating toward the truth inside you before you are capable of releasing the wrath but it does happen. The goal is not to become a 'bliss ninny' happy happy happy all the time.

The endgame is extending your parameters of what it means for you to be in this gift of life.

Now you understand how repetition works. Repetition works to emphasize and enhance neuronal patterns. Since repetition is necessary to build or re-route neuronal pathways, meditation must be practiced repetitively in order to re-wire the neuronal pathways.

This repetition is called ritual and it has another power. The latest science tells us ritual empowers an activity, or language, to the point of it being a placebo. And the world of placebo research will help us understand the power of repetition in meditation.

But first, the meditation.

~

How to Practice Meditation

Recall the research reported by Marco Iacoboni, in *Mirroring People*. He states "...solid, empirical evidence suggests that our brains are capable of mirroring the deepest aspects of the minds of others—intention is definitely one such aspect—at the fine-grained level of a *single brain cell.*" (2008, p. 7).

As we shall see it does not matter whether the person is living, or a child's doll, smaller by far or larger than we are, our brains receive the intention and begin growing neural pathways in mimicry.

Sacred Space: A Place to Meditate

To begin a meditation practice, find a place in your home. A separate room is best, or a place where no one will disturb you. Some people find that a closed door is not quite enough, so they write a small note, do not disturb for instance, to put on the door when meditating.

Take a bit of time to prepare the space. You may know you are going to be more comfortable sitting on a chair rather than on the floor. If so, put the chair in the room. It is best if the chair is dedicated to the purpose of meditation and not one that may be used for other people, other circumstances. However, do what you can with what you have on hand. Know that your intention to create a sacred space is what matters.

Take care to add some beauty to the room, perhaps a vase of live flowers or a pleasant picture. A window that opens onto a quiet, natural setting, even a single tree adds to a feeling of being grounded.

Recall that our deepest emotions leave impressions on whatever space we occupy. When you meditate continually your meditation space will begin to hold the energy of your intended calm and serenity and will begin to act as a mental "nest" to which you may return, especially when life gets difficult.

Altars

Many people like to construct an altar in their meditation space. This can be as simple as a small table with a photo of someone who holds spiritual power for you, and/or a flower, stone or some item that feels sacred to you.

I was given a piece of driftwood years ago from Manitoulin Island, a spiritual gathering place about 7 hours by car from where I live. I like to have it on any altar I make because it reminds me of the sacredness of the natural world.

I like to change my altars, sometimes place a Buddha statue in my living room to hold my rosary, called a mala rather than keep all my altar sites in my meditation space. You may play with this part of meditation preparation to your heart's content.

Altars are not all indoors. You may discover a peaceful place in nature where you feel supported and comfortable. If so, establish yourself in a comfortable posture and open to the power of the natural world.

Meditation Time

Now that we have looked at space let's consider time. You may want to experiment with this to discover if you meditate best in the morning or the evening. Sometimes morning energy is too full and wants physical expression so meditating at that time goes against the grain of the body's natural timing.

Sometimes later in the evening causes an upbeat energy

that interferes with sleep. Figure out through experimentation what time within your daily cycle works best for you.

Now make yourself a promise you will keep to this time, to the best of your ability.

Make the time specific, such as 7 a.m. or 7 p.m. and consistent.

Know that you will fail. Understand this. Failing in meditation is exactly the same as failing anywhere else in life—it signals that you are ready to start again.

This effort of starting and starting again is so deeply ingrained in meditation practice that a Zen master called Shunryu Suzuki wrote an entire book called *Zen Mind, Beginner's Mind* expressing just that.

Because meditation involves growing awareness of consciousness and consciousness is unbound, truly endless, every meditation session opens up a truly new beginning. Every meditator at every session begins again, anew.

Now how do you develop the habit of meditation so that it becomes a natural part of your daily life? You do this in the same way you create any new habit. It takes about 3 weeks of daily practice if you do not miss one day, to rewire your brain into accepting the new pattern of life.

It may take longer, perhaps 6 or 8 weeks, even more to "seal" the behaviour of getting to your meditation space and sitting, but with continued effort one day you will recognize how natural and easy the flow of your life is toward this daily behaviour. Through re-wiring your brain the new behaviour, called meditation will begin to feel natural.

What do I mean by re-wiring? Neurons, those trillions of nerves that dance with tiny electric stimuli inside our skulls have a particular tendency. When one neuron begins to light up, it nudges other neurons to do the same. Those neurons nudge others and soon lots of neurons light up in a pathway that grows from being like a foot path to being like the Auto

Bahn. This is the enactment of the mantra of neuroscientists: Neurons that fire together, wire together.

That means the more you do of something, the more likely you are to do it and the easier it becomes. You will in time notice that your mind begins to calm in readiness for the time you meditate. You are training your mind and it feels good!

I recommend starting with a shorter period of time and working your way in 5-minute intervals to a longer and longer course. Stabilize each 5-minute increase for at least a month before adding another 5 minutes.

When you are meditating and holding a job, raising a family, helping the elderly in your circle, it is best to plan on a total of no more than 45 mins per day.

Start with 5 minutes per session. If you truly know that is not enough, go for 15 but no more than 20 minutes to start. Then make yourself sit for 20 minutes no more, no less.

No more? Why would meditating more not be good for you?

Meditating past the time you have set encourages instability in meditation practice. It encourages the part of you that resists meditation to think, "Oh, I meditated more yesterday, so I'll meditate less today." Many tricks exist in the mind that resists!

Sometimes, and this can happen quite soon after beginning to meditate, you find time itself begins to shift: sometimes it seems that 5 minutes is at least an hour long and other times it feels like one breath.

For this reason you keep to the timing you have set for yourself. That way you always know the day world sense of timing even if your internal sense of time bends.

Therefore, establish a workable amount of time, a span that is reasonable given the family, work, hobbies and other involvements in your life and begin with this amount of time.

Meditation done in this way increases the strength in your conscious mind. It eventually allows you to decide instantly that shouting back at someone, no matter how desperately they may be deserving of it, is not the best course of action. It strengthens your ability to be less impulsive, more thoughtful in all areas of your life. In short, meditation practiced this way supports consciousness. Your daily mind of decision making grows in confidence and stability.

Keeping to the timing in your meditation, no matter which way the energy flows that day, good or bad, strengthens your capacity to keep the conscious mind making conscious decisions in your favour.

When you have established this amount of time steadily for a few months, you may want to increase it by 5 minutes. As soon as you do, you'll notice how your mind now leaps to make other exceptions. Hold to the extra five minutes and soon this scattered energy will settle down.

Finally bring a clock or old-fashioned watch, (not an iphone—too much temptation!) bring some paper or a journal and pens and set them beside your chosen place to sit or lie.

~

Pre-Meditation Moments

What? More ritual? Yes. Preparing your body to sit for a meditation session takes just a few minutes but makes a difference in your meditation experience. And ritual, as we have seen in the discussion about placebos, helps empower our practice.

Whenever you have the chance, take a short walk, 10 minutes will do nicely, before you sit in meditation. Leave ear buds and all electronics behind and focus lightly on your breath and body as you walk.

If walking outside is not possible, stretch. Stretch gently through your body trying to get all parts of your body from fingers and toes through to internal organs involved. Any form of gentle exercise such as Tai Chi, or yoga stretching is fine.

In general, it is best to avoid incense in the room where you will be meditating. A clean, quiet space, with minimum chance of distraction, phones etc off, excess lights from devices off, with a window open a small crack to let in fresh air is the best.

If these conditions don't exist, simply do your best.

∽

Posture

Many students ask about the correct posture. Before we go into ideas concerning posture, a word about preparing your body for meditation.

The idea of posture contains a long list of details: whether to sit or stand or lie, whether to sit on a chair, on a meditation cushion, or on the floor, whether to…and is best looked at now, because if you don't for sure the questions will come up once you begin to meditate.

Now that you have prepared with a bit of movement and gentle focusing on your breathing, deepening it to bring in more oxygen, sit in meditation.

For many people the cross-legged posture called Full

Vajra is unattainable. Good news! You do not need to pretzel your legs in order to gain benefit from meditation!

That posture, seen in many pictures of yogis, provides a kind of physical stability for meditators who are in full retreat. During full retreat waves of energy may fire up through the body and the body may contort in a number of ways, as held energies are released. No need for this posture when you're working a full week and juggling children, partners, family, homes.

Of course, this body movement often happens with emotional release as past terrors, rages and hurts course through and out of your body. Based on even a full hour per day, the energy will probably not be strong enough to send you out of your chosen posture.

If a chair feels best for you, sit in a chair. Keep your spine comfortably straight, what in yoga is called Natural Spine, with the gentle curves in it. In other words, not too rigid.

If the floor feels best, then lie on the floor.

Our culture provides almost no place and time to really relax. Therefore, when I taught meditation at the local yoga studio, I encouraged people to lie on the floor, on their yoga mat or snuggled under a blanket.

Our rule was you may fall asleep but if you snore, I will tweak your toe until you come back to the room!

Most of the time this worked comfortably for the majority of people. Many students found that the half hour provided them with a gentle easing, a deepening of relaxation they welcomed heartily.

Some students reported that with weekly practice of only half an hour, their general sense of calm stability increased throughout the rest of the week, even into work and family areas of struggle.

The best posture in general allows for your spine to be

gently straight, so your lungs may expand and contract easily. If you are sitting make sure you begin with your chin tucked in a tiny bit, just very gently toward your throat. This straightens the back of your neck and allows better breathing.

With your chin gently tucked and your spine in natural pose, you're all set.

You have begun to practice the mantra and its syllables (or repeat the Hail Mary prayer for example). Now you have one more instruction.

Mantra. Learn to repeat the syllables of the mantra by heart. Reciting the mantra as you gaze on the figure of Medicine Buddha completes the essence of the meditation.

Repeat. Repeat and repeat. Okay that's three but for as long as you have determined your meditation practice will be, 20 minutes or longer, you return again and again to visualizing in detail and saying aloud the mantra.

While you do this, you may find cynical voices rebounding through your mind eager to have you get up and do something useful, such as take out the garbage, clean the dishes.

Just watch and be aware. Now turn your mind back to what you have decided to meditate upon. You, in your conscious mind have made a decision. You in your conscious mind will not be moved. That is the essence instruction and teaching of all meditation.

If you are using a figure like Medicine Buddha, spend some time exploring the details of the figure. If you can, do this as you would examine the details of a beloved newborn. With curiosity and gentle love, take in as much as you can.

For instance, when it comes to the bowl in Medicine Buddha, try sitting with your left hand at your belly, imagining a bowl sitting on your open palm. How does this feel?

Keep reciting the mantra. Mantra: "man=mind" and "tra=tool" so mantra is a mind tool. Seen in this way, mantra, the repetitious saying aloud of certain words or syllables provides a tool. The tool is to help keep discursive thoughts (the lists of what you will do next, or should be doing, the moments from yesterday that linger, fantasies about the future, all of these are called discursive thoughts).

If you feel drawn to the Sanskrit mantra offered with the Medicine Buddha practice outline, one way to apply Reflective meditation practice to the mantra is to take one word. This one word becomes your anchor throughout the day. Repeat it mentally whenever and wherever you go.

The following list of Medicine Buddha's mantra syllables provides you with a starting point. You may go online to hear several versions of how to say the words and how they sound.

TAYATA, OM BEKADZE BEKADZE
MAHA BEKADZE BEKADZE,
RADZA SAMUNGATE
SOHA

This is pronounced:

Tie-ya-tar, om beck-and-zay beck-and-zay
ma-ha beck-and-zay beck-and-zay
run-zuh sum-oon-gut-eh
so-ha.

Now choose one word and take that one word with your throughout your day, repeating it as often as possible. It is fine for the repetition to be internal as circumstances do not always allow for this practice to be out loud.

If you like the English translation and wish to use one of these words, this also works. The efficiency of any practice does not depend upon the outer form, such as whether the words are in Sanskrit or English. What matters is the state of consciousness of the practitioner.

Having an open mind, but one curious to discover truth is extremely helpful.

From www.landofmedicinebuddha.org/about-medicine-buddha/meaning-of-mantra-and-praise/
we find this helpful guidance:

Tayatha – means "like this".

Om – is composed of the three pure sounds A U and MA, which signifies one's own body, speech and mind that get transformed into the vajra holy body, speech and mind.

Then bekandze bekandze -"eliminating pain, eliminating pain". What eliminates pain is medicine. This pain is not ordinary pain – even animals do not want to experience that. The first eliminating pain is true suffering, the second is the true cause of suffering. The medicine that eliminates pain is first the graduated path of the lower capable being, and second the graduated path of the middle capable being.

Then maha bekandze -"the great eliminating pain" is the graduated path of the higher capable being, which eliminates the subtle defilements.

So bekandze bekandze maha bekandze contains the whole path to enlightenment, the ultimate medicine.

Radza – is king.

Samudgate – (ocean of goodness)

Soha – to establish the foundation in the heart, the blessing, the devotion from which the realization comes.

Understanding that Medicine Buddha applies most clearly to the suffering created by hatred, greed and delusion, called the Three Poisons, helps us understand why our emotions may rise to the surface when doing this meditation practice.

Other benefits come with practice. You grow accustomed to listening to your voice and gradually you find it easier and easier to speak your thoughts in the world. While in meditation you may find your voice spontaneously dropping to a whisper or sometimes rising in tone and volume. Just go with it as far as you can.

As you remember to focus on the figure of Medicine Buddha and as you commit to learning the syllables and sounds of the mantra your mind focuses. When your mind wanders (and even with all this learning and sound going on, your mind will wander into discursive thought) the visualization and mantra repetitions become the anchors to bring you back to the present moment.

This strengthens your mind for daily life, empowering as it does the part of you that is steady, focused, balanced and aware.

It is that simple, and that challenging as anyone who has tried to establish a daily meditation practice knows.The three keys to achieving a daily meditation practice are this— keep trying, keep trying and keep trying.

And this brings us to our next focus on how and why meditation on imagined figures works: placebos.

But before we go there, we look at how to end a meditation session.

How to Close A Meditation Session

Since as you are aware by now the point of meditation is to practice awareness it is important to continue awareness right through to the very end of the very end of your session. This means a structure for how to close.

Remember you are training your conscious mind to stay online despite urges to quickly get up. It is important, unless your house is on fire, to remain in the calm you have generated for a few minutes after you finish the meditation practice. This allows your conscious mind to return fully to your own body, feel any changes perhaps tingling or tiredness, maybe energization or emotional waves.

As you come to the time when your meditation must end stop for a moment. Recognize how your mind reverberates with the sound of the mantra and the vision of Medicine Buddha or the spiritual teacher of your choice. Notice and stay silent and still.

As these reverbs cease it is time to offer the merit.

Recall the meditation in as much detail as possible. Next take the pen and paper and write a few notes, no more than about 5 lines worth, of details you recall.

Next, offer the merit. In Western terms, merit means simply that you have done a good deed. By trying to meditate you have made effort to improve yourself and in that to improve life for everyone. Now this good energy is dedicated to helping all life in all directions. That is the Western meaning.

Merit in Tibetan Buddhism means a pool of energy. It is acquired so the pool grows larger by wholesome thoughts words and speech. For more on the Tibetan Buddhist ideas around merit and how to increase merit look up the Paramis.

I am fond of the short sharing of merit chant in Tibetan. A short article on the meaning and experience of sharing merit comes from The Lion's Roar an online magazine. From that article here are two possible English language prayers of dedication of merit:

> *Through this goodness may awakening spontaneously arise in our streams of being. May all obscurations and distortions fall away. May all beings be liberated from suffering, and the stormy waves of birth, sickness, old age, and death.*
>
> *By this merit may all attain omniscience. May it defeat the enemy, wrong-doing. From the stormy waves of birth, old age,*

sickness, and death, from the ocean of samsara, may I free all beings.

My own practice includes chanting to the best of my ability the Tibetan words—

Idam te punna kamman asavakkhaya vaham hotu

I was taught it is impossible to say the same mantra twice, so I just pronounce the words as best I can.

What happens with this dedication is the mind turns toward offering. Why offer? It is a gentle reminder of the suffering of others. This alone is a simple and effective way of reducing the self-orientation prevalent in our society.

Having experienced meditation whether you struggled and felt strong difficult emotions (even one hour a day may promote this kind of healing from the Depth) or sailed along in a comforting and sustaining cloud of well-being (again experiences that may rise with surprisingly little meditation practice) at this point you remember all the beings who suffer because life is difficult. You offer to them whatever empowering energy has come to you from this experience. In this way you subtly train the mind toward oneness of all life.

That thought generates compassion and in this state of compassion you may dwell for a moment or two.

Dissolving What Has Been Created

The last moment involves dissolving what you have created. You have produced, through your mind, a medically helpful, and emotionally supportive image. You have spent time, 20 minutes to 45 minutes, engaging with this figure created through your imagination. Now as a gesture of how real the figure is and therefore how substantial the benefits flowing towards you, you dissolve the figure.

You may focus again on the figure and mantra, snap fingers of both hands and believe the entire creation dissolves. You may say the Tibetan phrase, "Benzra Mu." This is a sound signifying dissolution.

You may choose to create a few words of your own, in whatever language feels comfortable to you. Those words may be along the line of "gone now, completely gone" or "everything empties into being dissolved." Use the words that feel best to you and believe fully.

~

Why Bother?

All this ritual, all this attention to detail just to sit and do what children do so easily, imagine something?

We know the power of our imaginations alone creates about 2/3rds of the same effect as if you were enacting a physical experience. (For the science on this see *The Healing Power of Mind* p.39)

Yes. The rituals and attention to detail create a super force in your brain that empowers your visualization. Remember: neurons that fire together, wire together. So, the more neurons you have going toward your meditation the greater the effect.

In Tibetan culture rituals known as Wongs may last several hours, even several days. Some Crown initiations may take an entire month!

Each detail of every day, or every hour of these elaborate ceremonies involves deepening and improving the intricacies of every step of the sacred empowerment. That's why the word Wong translates as Empowerment: having doused your brain for days and weeks in focused concentration on the meditation practice, your daily meditation opens up much more easily. It is easier to pay attention and to direct the power of your attention where you want it to go.

CHAPTER 8

*A*pplying Meditation to Daily Life

Autogenic Training

Find a comfortable position. Now focus on your feet. Bring your awareness to the inside of your feet. Linger for a moment, imagining the ligaments, tendons, flesh and bones that live inside the skin on your feet.

In a few breaths move up to your ankles. Repeat the lingering exercise, this time focusing on your ankle bones. Notice how precisely your ankle bones interlock to provide the kind of flexibility you need.

Again for your calves, knees, thighs, and so on. Continue up your back and the back of your neck, across your shoulders and down your arms into your hands. And back.

Now come up the back of your head to the crown, then down to your forehead.

Linger around your eyes, releasing some of the held

tension there. Then move your focus to include your cheeks and jaw muscles, then your lips.

And remember to include your tongue.

Begin the practice and with time you'll find it releases more tension. You might also find in time that you include more details like each toe, each finger, each digit and so on.

A second version includes syncing with your breath and is excellent for those nights when sleep seems reluctant to arrive.

You begin with your feet, as above, but scrunch your feet tightly as you inhale, hold for 2 or 3 seconds then release breath and muscles together at once. Ahhhh!

Take the breath throughout your body in this way, taking in a relaxed and gentle inhale with each muscle scrunch.

Complete a cycle then return again to your feet.

~

Your Belly Has a GPS

In our time many people feel lost about how to make good life decisions. Bookshelves bulge with writings about how to make better life decisions, from business books, to life coaching books to books about relationships and inner growth. Some of these books may prove helpful but what you have inside you is a fool proof way of discovering for yourself what decisions to make about every aspects of your life: relationships, business, even health and meditation practices.

The story goes that a CEO of Sony was asked how he had made successful business decisions amassing a great fortune over his lifetime. He replied, "I take the decision into my mouth and chew it. If it tastes bad, I spit it out and will not go forward with the proposal. If it tastes good, I swallow and see how it feels in my stomach. If it feels good, it's a yes. If not I abandon the idea."

Our bodies' intelligence has been denied and denigrated for centuries. We know very little about the intelligence that keeps us safe from harm, that guides us and knows this planet better than our intellects will ever do.

Inside our bellies lies an intelligence that acts like a GPS. This system is so fine-tuned you may use it for future events as well as present day decisions.

Take a few moments to relax. You might put one hand on your chest and one on your belly then breathe gently for 3 minutes or so.

Now look at a calendar or imagine an event you know is coming up in the next while. How far away or how close the event may be does not matter. It may be tomorrow, or it may be months in the future.

Feel how you feel in your body, specifically your belly, when you imagine or consider this event.

If you feel good, the event holds something for you that will be of benefit.

If you feel a sinking feeling in your energy, as though you are suddenly tired or disinterested the event holds nothing that will help you in your life.

Even if the event looks to all purposes to be something that will help you, sustain, guide or support you or your business, if you feel this drop in energy the event has nothing to offer you.

Finally, if you feel nothing, neither a drop nor an upbeat in energy and the event is far off in time, try it again closer to the time of the actual experience.

You can put this to the test. If you discover an event that

your body, especially your stomach tells you beforehand will cause a drop in your energy and you go, see if your body/stomach told you the truth. You can gather the data for yourself.

If you see an event or date that does not look promising on the surface but for which your body/stomach brings you an uptick go and find out for yourself.

Keep a small chart somewhere, perhaps in your day journal or calendar that will give you the information you need to begin making decisions based on what your stomach/body have to say about the situation.

In this way you may feel increased confidence about making decisions that are correct for you, right for your life. From this you will conserve energy and have more energy to bring to those experiences which will help guide, support, protect and help you on your way to health, enough wealth, positive relationships and more.

∾

The Blue Egg

Our lives move quickly, time seems to have been compressed and sometimes we need an instant way to feel more grounded, and more protected in order to respond in a way that will reduce suffering, for ourselves and others.

An example may be a relative. You and others in your family may acknowledge this person is troublesome, difficult, hard to get along with or you may feel singled out to receive the most negative part of this person's behaviour.

It does not matter. When you are about to meet with family and your know this person will attend, prepare with the Blue Egg.

First, find your feet. Focus on the soles of your feet as they connect to the floor or wherever.

Next, visualize yourself within a dark blue sphere. The blue is the colour of a midnight sky without stars, blue almost into black but definitely blue. This sphere shaped like an egg with the narrow end at top surrounds you about 3 feet out from your skin.

The shell of this egg contains material so strong nothing, not a thing in any Universe can penetrate it. You are sheltered, protected, in refuge within this beautiful calming Egg.

Dwell in this inner sanctum letting yourself feel the effects of being utterly protected. Dwell on being protected such that nothing, even a tsunami, even a raging fire can penetrate the shell of this egg.

Practice this as you go about your day whether or not you feel endangered.

Then, when you know you will be encountering someone who provides you with difficulty, apply the Blue Egg to protect yourself.

This works on numerous occasions including with a troublesome boss or superior at work, family member, acquaintance or even when you are sitting alone and thinking about a person who bothers you. Do not dwell in the negative but apply the Blue Egg.

~

Peach Feet Meditation

We often wish to have achieved more. Whether we desire better health, more knowledge, more money, better relationships or anything else, we feel the urge to gain what we feel separated from.

This exercise allows you to feel connected to a form of yourself that has already achieved what you so wish to attain.

You may focus on one item, however it is best done through a general sense. The general sense of having what you wish, of fulfilling the person you wish to be is enough to help you relax into becoming that.

This exercise supports a sense of confidence and well-being. Lie on your back. It is helpful to dim the lights but if this makes you uncomfortable, leave the lights on.

Now put one hand on your belly and one on your chest around the heart centre. Breathe naturally letting your breath go where it will, how it will for 3-5 minutes.

When you feel calm and grounded in your skin, imagine your body fills with peach-coloured light. Start at your head and move through, just suggesting to yourself that peach-coloured light is filling each section of your body and remaining there as you move to the next part.

It is not necessary to be able to visualize. Simply suggest to yourself this is what is happening. In time and with practice you may discover how to visualize but it is not necessary for this to work on consciousness.

Now as you reach your feet having filled every part of your body with peach-coloured light discover another body seamed to yours by the soles of your feet.

This body lies directly opposite yours and is the true form of your exemplary self. All the qualities you wish to obtain, this form has already achieved. Dwell in connection with the idealized self.

You may use this to help with health issues, employment struggles, confidence, making money, relationships, love—any issue you may think of this form has attained. Dwell with this attainment.

∾

Breathe!

Another simple but very important practice that, once incorporated into you as habit will enhance your daily life immeasurably is breathing. Take a few minutes as often as possible to just breathe. Pull your shoulders back, open your belly and breathe.

This can be done at an office desk, while taking a noon walk, in the living room while watching tv, in your bed, literally anywhere. Just turn your focus toward your breath and breathe.

~

One Sense a Day

The effect of meditation is to increase awareness. Awareness involves opening and developing our senses. Another method for bringing meditation into your daily is the following.

Take one sense per day, or week, to focus upon as a meditation practice. For instance, if you decide to focus on hearing use this as your meditation anchor. Focus on sound throughout your day. If you live in the city the sound of traffic, people walking and talking perhaps shouting, may be dominant.

If you live with someone else notice how the sound of their voice affects you. This works with four-legged companions as well.

Notice the sounds and notice also where in your body the sounds register. With practice you will learn that sound registers throughout your body not just in your ears and head.

Jot down your experiences in your meditation journal as detailed in the first section of this book.

Take your tactile sense of textures on your skin, then smell and then taste. Use your eyes as meditation focus last, because the best way to experience your eyes is to rest them.

Offering Negativity, Disease or Unhappy States

Another exercise is to identify a particular disease, or your fear of a particular disease or of disease in general and offer it to Medicine Buddha.

Open your meditation as usual. Now visualize Medicine Buddha in front of you. He sits on a lotus and moon disc which hover steadily at about your hairline.

Visualize his body as larger than yours. From our physiological experiments cited above we know this will encourage in you an increased sense of spaciousness, which will also suggest a deepening of your breathing pattern.

Now put the disease or fear you have in mind up into Medicine Buddha until you feel or sense that he has it. It is no longer on earth. Take time to visualize what the world might look like without this disease. How many more happy, healthy people feel safe and vital in their lives, helping others to feel the same? Sense the uplift to the entire earth's energy sphere.

Close your meditation with the usual sharing of merit and dissolution practices as above.

Eyes Right!

Our world is eye dominant. Although many people now turn to podcasts and audio books and in this exercise their ears, we remain in a world where our eyes dominate. Computers, reading, looking out a window, every moment of our waking day relies upon our eyes.

Yet we seldom think to offer our eyes respite. In his remarkable book *The Brain's Way of Healing* Dr. Norman Doidge reveals his discussion with David Webber, a man blind from the age of 43. Of what he discovered through being blind, David states, "I learned that vision is much more than simply seeing details and reading symbols...it is my whole self that sees, not the eyes" (2015, p. 199).

Consider. If you see with your whole body and you want to rest your eyes, it makes sense to relax your entire system.

Support for this knowledge comes a few pages later, when Doidge writes, "...William Bates...knew...the extent to which stress can affect the body, the muscles and their tone, and the eyes (where adrenaline enlarges the pupil, affects circulation, and increases internal pressure)" (2015, p.202).

For more on Bates' method of improving eyesight https://www.goodreads.com/book/show/ 1045071.The_Bates_Method_for_Better_Eyesight_without _Glasses

Because the four eye relaxation responses are so well written in Doidge's famous book *The Brain's Way of Healing*, I offer them directly from the source.

David Webber's experience included asking his meditation teacher Lesley George Dawson, for help.

Dawson, who is quoted in Doidge's book as the source of these ancient eye exercises said,

Meditate on the colour blue-black for a few hours a day. It is the colour of the midnight sky, the only colour that will totally and completely relax the muscles of the eyes, that is the most important thing. In the past, this method had healed even shattered eyes. Try lying on your back with your feet flat on the floor, knees pointed to the ceiling, with your hands resting quietly on your belly. (2015, p. 207).

For most of us a shorter time will help the eyes relax. You might try 10 minutes and gradually expand this as time allows.

Doidge continues,

This posture would reduce tension in the lower back and in the neck and would also allow for less restricted breathing. While doing this meditation...put...palms on (your) eyes to further relax them. But the emphasis of this visualization meditation was to achieve 'a quiet, spacious-feeling state of mind...

Second, Namgyal Rinpoche told him to "move the eyes up, down, left, and right, and around in circles, as well as on the diagonals."

Third, he said he must "blink frequently."

And fourth, he said, "Sun your eyes. Sit at a forty-five-degree angle to the sun, in the morning or later afternoon when the sun is lower in the sky, eyes closed to let the warmth and light penetrate through all the eye tissues, like taking a warm bath for the eyes, ten to twenty minutes a day. (2015, p.207).

Vagus Nerve Calming: For the feeling of Comfort

The vagus nerve is a bundle of nerves running from your brain stem to touch every organ of your body. This bundle relays messages from the state of those organs and your body in general back up to the brain.

From there, the brain sends signals to the Vagus nerve.

Most of us live in a state of hyperarousal where the Sympathetic Nervous System is on too much. To balance this state of fight, flight or freeze here is a simple exercise. It will bring your Parasympathetic Nervous System online within 5 minutes.

Simply place one hand on your heart area and the other hand on your stomach. Then breathe naturally for 3 to 5 minutes. This will change your state of being to one of calm relaxation.

Singing

Singing changes the state of your neural pathways no matter what state they are in! So sing softly or loudly, let your musical self fill a room or only let out a tiny whisper whenever you want to shift your brain to a more positive, uplifting set of pathways.

Large and Small

Every morning at 3 am when he rises, His Holiness the Dalai Lama stands outside and gazes up at the stars and universes spreading out. He says this practice helps him remember he is less than a speck on a tiny planet circling a sun that is almost invisibly small compared to our closest neighbour star, Arcturus.

Consider—Jupiter is large enough to contain 1,500 planets the size of Earth!

When you have thoughts that will not leave, it is helpful to know how to put everything into perspective.

Click on National Geographic's images of the relative size of planets in our solar system. Take a good look at how small Earth looks beside the giants Jupiter and Saturn.

Then enter in your browser for more perspective. How big is Jupiter in comparison to say, the nearest Red Giant, called Arcturus.

Then look at some of the fabulous images available for Arcturus and its massive size compared to our Sun.

Turn back to realize Earth is quite small compared to our Sun. And the Sun is small compared to our closest Red Giant Star.

Now put your struggles, problems, recurring thoughts on the tiny spec of Earth where you stand, and gaze out, or pretend to gaze out, to Jupiter, Saturn and on to Arcturus.

Play like this expands our minds and helps us keep a perspective that leads to mental and emotional balance.

CHAPTER 9

*C*onclusions

We have learned how vitally important our faith is to creating the best result from whatever path or pill to healing we decide upon. We have come to understand how our brains respond to the idea that a substance will help us, even when that substance is known to be inert.

We have heard from scientists and researchers, doctors and naturopaths about the dimly understood good health results that arise from having faith and belief in what you are doing to improve your health.

And everything we have learned describes exactly how meditating on figures and intoning sounds helps our brains mimic the intention of those figures. When we meditate on a healing icon such as Medicine Buddha, whose posture displays health and healing for all diseases, we ourselves promote the multitude of healing hormones and miracle molecules with which our bodies are blessed.

Practiced regularly, visualization meditation does lead to increased calm stability, increased serenity and increased life enjoyment. Even the down times feel less heavy, less weighty when you know you can turn to a colourful, serene and uplifting visualization.

Now we know how our brains work to provide us with this result from simply spending time looking at the figure of another and making sounds. Western science has proven the ancient techniques of Tibetan Buddhist Vajrayana Tantra works to help heal our lives.

The road to this takes patience and much determination. And you will discover emotional struggles you thought you had put behind you. Without doubt you will have to learn to sit through many emotions as they rise. And fall.

And, just like breath, your emotional content no matter how intense in the moment will rise to a peak and fall again.

This was one of the first and most lasting and valuable lessons I was taught in my early 20's by the insightful meditation teacher Cecilie Kwiat.

All emotion rises as a wave. If you endure it until the wave has peaked, while you watch for the ending of the wave, the intensity will subside. And it will, always subside, safely and without the use of medicine.

Cecilie traveled with Dawson, aka Namgyal Rinpoche, as did I and, while Cecilie went on to become a globe-traveling meditation teacher and emotional guide, I became a householder therapist and meditation teacher in my hometown.

Still the work has to be done. The work of clearing and cleansing consciousness is never over. It has been the work of my life and now, my honour to offer to you this book, the second in the series Mind Medicine.

For more on meditation and healing look into *The Healing Power of Mind: Medicine Buddha Medicine Mind.*
mybook.to/medicinebuddhamind

It is the first in the series Mind Medicine.

If you enjoy fiction, consider *The Stain—A Book of Reincarnation, Karma and the Release from Suffering.*

mybook.to/TheStain

And for inspiration on defeating challenges in life read my award-winning memoir *My Impossible Life—trauma travel & transcendence.*

mybook.to/myimpossiblelife

getbook.at/myimpossiblelife

It is my hope that suffering may soon be relinquished, and all may experience living in physical, mental and emotional well-being.

∽

CHAPTER 10

*C*M ore by Charlene Jones M.Ed/M.A.

If you enjoyed *Medicine Mind Buddha Mind* don't miss the first in the series Mind Medicine

The Healing Power of Mind: Medicine Buddha Medicine Mind
  Excerpt—
  A Brief History of Vajrayana Tantra
  A Trace of Mysticism

The legendary Shaman and Teacher Padmasambhava traveled out of his native India sometime in the 8th century ACE to the wild northern lands known as Tibet. There he encountered a kind of mysticism based on what we might think of today as Voodoo: the power of casting spells, the powers of magic. This mysticism was called Bon.

Because the Bon tradition with its ritual incantations and spell making already existed, Padmasambhava, eager to convert these Tibetans to the new way of living called Buddhism, took major aspects of the Bon ceremonies and wove those with his profound insight into the teachings of the Buddha who had lived in India over a hundred centuries prior.

The insight of Padmasambhava, that cultures are most easily persuaded toward a new religion through similarities to the old one, echoes our knowledge of the Pre-Christ roots of Christianity. In Zoroastrianism, a star above a humble shed, some members of the elite journeying toward a new infant, shepherds on watch noticing fantastic events unfolding in the night sky, all blend into our story of Christ's birth.

Padmasambhava's legendary mysticism fell upon my ears this way. A Teacher may speak about the history of the Wong. The history opens a peek into the mythological or perhaps real history of that initiation ceremony, that specific Wong. Namgyal Rinpoche before entering with us into the Wong of Padmasambhava, revealed some of the stories surrounding this legendary figure.

Padmasambhava traveled through Tibet and came across a tavern, rolls one such story. Being thirsty he entered the humble building. We imagine the native Tibetans seeing this man from India with his strange clothes, peculiar hair and odd habits. We may imagine suspicion and a restless sense of danger rising among the customers and bartender.

Padmasambhava asks for a drink. The bartender, taking note of the change in the air, the tension in the faces around him, says, "Nothing here for you."

Padmasambhava repeats his request. The bartender again refuses. A third time.

Padmasambhava slides from its sheath his purba, (a ceremonial curved knife reputed to destroy demons) slams it into the wooden bar, crying, "Then the sun will not set until you do!"

Customers mumble among themselves, some mocking, sneering at this upstart with his outrageous claims. The more superstitious glance with growing anxiety toward the oddly dressed stranger and beyond him, the sun.

As the first day passes into night, then the second, and the sun stays in the same spot, others from the countryside having heard through the grapevine of these happenings begin to filter into the tiny tavern. Some beg the bartender to reconsider. Their flocks, herds and domestic animals, their wives are upset and complaining and they themselves feel the dread upon the land of this supernatural experience.

Finally, on the third day the bartender pours the drink, imploring Padmasambhava, "Let the sun set! Only let the sun set!" He puts the drink in front of the great Mystic and the sun does what the sun is supposed to do.

When I first heard it, I enjoyed this story for its mythological size and content. I did not believe it. Namgyal Rinpoche bestowed the Guru Rinpoche Empowerment (the Padmasambhava Wong) more than once, each time revealing another aspect of Padmasambhava's miraculous powers and his predictions.

Padmasambhava left a legacy of predictions, one of the most famous being, "When the Iron Horse runs on tracks and the Silver Bird flies, the Tibetan people will be scattered across the Earth like ants." This translates easily into the understanding that when trains run along the ground and airplanes fly the Tibetan diaspora will begin. Check.

Padmasambhava went on to describe some of the events to come in what is known as the "Kali Yuga" or our current times. Kali refers to the Hindi Goddess of Time, Change and Destruction. A Yuga is an unimaginably long time.

Padmasambhave predicted mass insanity with mass murders taking place for no reason.

Certainly prior to our times and likely during the times of Padmasambhava mass executions delivered with a sense of revenge, perhaps even a feeling of justice by many who felt insulted, disobeyed, ripped off, in short poorly treated, took place.

What this Mystic's predication stated was that the increase in numbers of mass killings would spring from no political turmoil, no religious fervour, no immediate cause save the insanity of the killer. Padmasambhava said mental illness would get bad enough that people in large cities would step over the dead bodies lying in the street, so immune would they be to death.

This happened during the Communist uprising in the '30's and '40's. My Russian mother-in-law remembered having to walk around a decomposing corpse lying on the street in her village after the Communists came and shot the person, presumably to send a message. The message was received: if you showed any response to the corpse, you too would be shot.

Padmasambhava's predictions outline a time when some, crying for help on the streets, would be greeted with blank stares and empty gazes from those passing by. Street people? The homeless?

If you enjoy inspirational memoirs detailing how meditation helps heal, you will enjoy

My Impossible Life trauma travel & transcendence

Excerpt—

September 1968

I slide into the new powder blue Pontiac, leaving bright autumn leaves, late summer air behind. Nothing can go wrong. I left in the dark the night before, hitchhiked out of my old life onto the black highway of this unknown. No longer compelled by dictates of parents, teachers, even friends, I am free to decide, free to do as I please. I am sixteen, everyone everywhere from commercials to pop songs to poems, promotes freedom and personal choice; it's my life and I am free.

Miles spin beneath as I stare at the blurred bushes and trees that line the TransCanada Highway, north of Sudbury. I lean my cheek against the cool window behind the driver.

"How far you planning to go?" The driver's watery blue eyes stare at me from the rear-view mirror, a slightly twisted grin on his soft, large lips.

"Edmonton." Into the small silence I add, "And you?"

"Oh, me and Gary, he's…" the driver nods in the direction of the handsome, swarthy young man whose brown eyes had hypnotized me into the car, in the front seat, "…he's Gary."

"He's Al," Gary responds as though this is rehearsed.

"We're just free, you know? We go wherever we want, don't we Gary?" Al chuckles without mirth.

I nod, "I know what you mean."

"Do you?" Al shoots back at me but glances at Gary. "What's your name?"

"Charlie."

"Charlie, Charlie," he repeats as though trying to remember something.

"What do you guys do for work?"

"What?" The word slices toward me. I see a taut snag at the corner of his mouth.

Gary absorbs Al's tension. "We just do whatever we feel like, don't we Al? We're free."

"That's right, Gar, just free to do what we want."

"That's us, free and easy."

"We just hang around, go wherever we want, right Gary?" Al repeats.

"That's right, Al." Gary looks out the window.

"We don't believe in being tied down, kept on other people's time, wasting our lives working for the man, that right Gary?"

"That's right, Al."

"What about money, what do you do for money?"

A short pause.

"You see that canvas bag back there?" Al, his watery eyes claiming mine, asks. "Well, that canvas bag contains two shot-guns. Gary here has sawed one off, right Gary?"

"Yes, I did Al," Gary nods shyly.

"Those shot-guns are the ones we used to shoot the legs out from under a gas station attendant in Welland, after we broke out of prison. You know where Welland is, Charlie?"

"Southwest of Toronto." Inside, all my pieces separate, fall away.

How does memory, released from the body, contain the potential to heal? Find out in *My Impossible Life trauma travel & transcendence* .

~

Do you ever wonder if you have lived before, in another time? Do you ever consider where you may be in future?

You'll enjoy The Stain, a work of Historical Fiction that explores the theme of past lives creating impact on present lives.

The Stain —A Book of Reincarnation, Karma & the Release from Suffering

Excerpt—

Mary's life, London England 1885

Mrs. Sheldrake, keeper of this home for the indigent and insane, eyed the small, brown skinned man in front of her. He was talking, but what she noted was his personal warmth, which felt to her very like hope. Hope rose in her heart as a ghost, dangerous, wailing, pulling bitter disappointment right behind. She curled against this, unconsciously lifting herself to her full height and leaning her body away from him. The man's voice pierced through to Mrs. Sheldrake's brain.

"Mary Eagleton is her name. I believe she was registered with you several months ago," he was saying. His different skin and gentlemanly demeanour provoked in Sheldrake a sense of high society which her own cockney accent denied.

"Yes, yes, I know the one you speak of. She's up on the rafters, that one." She raised her eyebrows, her wrinkled face following the gesture until every line moved toward her greasy, grey hair.

"Yes, I'm sure it's been difficult," he acknowledged. "Here, if you would be so kind as to accept this…" and the small, soft palm of the gentleman opened depositing a few shillings into her own hand, although she did not recall offering it to him.

"Of course you must want to see her yourself, you've come such a long way." Mrs. Sheldrake's assumption, that the gentleman had travelled great distances from an exotic point of origin, provoked from her the use of formal names. "She'll be in the Recreation Room."

He turned silently and followed her through to a heavy

door which she unlocked using a key from many dangling from the large metal ring at the side of her apron. They stepped a short way down a dark, narrow hallway when she beckoned with her hand that he look through a small, barred window on a door to his right.

People, maybe twenty, some shuffling slowly around the perimeter, any number of them moaning, or shouting suddenly, populated this dark den. Three small high windows on the opposite side opened directly to the elements. Years of snow and rain had flooded portions of the room and now moss grew beneath those far windows as though to remind those on this side of the green growing life outside. Yet no eye might take comfort by looking at trees or grass because the opening was too high. Only a scrap of sky for any who looked up, a scrap of sky and the moss, green and damp, lining the wall in a dingy, downward pattern.

No one looked in any case. They walked slowly, or rocked themselves or leaned against the walls, staring off to some other place, another time, or to nothing at all.

Mipham, whose native land India with its many meditation masters had afforded him training in observation, focus and attention, instantly absorbed the entire scene. His eyes however never stopped searching for Mary.

The former beauty huddled against the back wall, swaying slightly, her eyes distant, unfocused. He took in the matted, unwashed hair, swollen, infected skin, and the curve of her arms around an invisible baby to which, as he walked closer, he heard her humming.

What Mary experienced was a sunlit meadow just beyond the trees she saw in her inner world. She was trying to get to the meadow, to that safe, warm place.

"Mary," he called softly. Then again, "Mary."

The thin veil of possible comfort receded as she heard her name. The last syllable of her name yanked the next,

Theodore, from her. Theodore who had loved her, Theodore whose child she had, Theodore gone from her, this name dredged with it an intolerable anguish.

"Theodo....ahrhg," the wail erupting from her thin body sounded part animal, part human, part from another dimension.

Mipham stepped back, reconfiguring. Clearly Theodore's callousness had cleaved her psyche more deeply than Mipham had understood. Now it was going to take time to bring her back, coax her back to the land of the living, "...if that is even possible," he thought. His training in meditation as a path to cure the mentally ill told him it was possible, but the depth of Mary's anguish and the loss of the child argued against it.

Mrs. Sheldrake, eager to ease this exotic and wealthy looking stranger's way, tried to soothe. "Now, now you didn't know she were as bad off as this...she comes and goes, she does and best left to being gone for all as ever 'appens is that wailing and moaning."

Her solid frame led Mipham back through the large door and out to the reception area.

"I'll come again, if that is quite all right," he said.

Anticipating the warm feel of shillings across her palm for whatever small favors she might apply to this man, Mrs. Sheldrake eagerly responded as her eyes followed her hand in replacing the key on its large ring, "Come as often as ye like, then. We'll take good care of her, our Mary, yes, we will, you can be sure of that, as best as..."

Mipham was already out the door.

For the next few visits he again crossed the sodden, grimy floor, stood a few feet away from Mary's side, watching. Mipham absorbed every detail including her breath, which came in and left from the top of her chest, stopping altogether for long periods of time. These two signs, her breath coming in and leaving through the top of her lungs, and the large gap between breaths demonstrated deep mental and emotional disturbance within the young woman.

He deliberately focused on his own breath, allowing it to come and go freely. Mary hummed, rocked her invisible baby, and stared toward the meadow only she could see.

～

Poetry for People Who Don't Like Poetry

Talking to Myself

Talking to myself used to be just fine,
    But now the voices in my head number eight or nine.
    To get a word in edgewise I have to stand in line.
    And there's nowhere left to sit
    And they've finished all the wine
    But they haven't washed the glasses
    And I'd like to kick some asses
    But I can't be certain
    Which of them are mine.

Linda Stitt
    For more of the incomparable Linda State get the ebook Talking to Myself.
    www.soulsciences.net

～

Bliss Pig, More Poetry for People Who Don't Like Poetry

By Linda Stitt and Charlene Jones
www.soulsciences.net

~

Uncritical Mass in Consort: Poetry by Linda Stitt, Cecilie Kwiat and Charlene Jones.

Reviews are author gold. Please consider leaving a few words of review on amazon, Barnes and Noble, Kobo, Goodreads or other reputable sites.

I'd enjoy hearing from you. Please contact me at charlenej@rogers.com

~

REFERENCES

*D*oidge, Norman. *The Brain That Changes Itself, Stories of*
Personal Triumph from the Frontiers of Brain Science,
Penguin 2007.
- - -The Brain's Way of Healing, *Remarkable*
Discoveries and Recoveries from the
Frontiers of Plasticity, 2015. Penguin Group, 2015.

Ehrsson, H. Henrik, Guterstam, Arvid, van der Hoort, Bjorn,
Being Barbie, The Size of One's Own Body Determines the
Perceived Size of the World, May 25, 2011, DOI:10:1371/
journal/pone/0020195 PLOS ONE.

Fisher, Nicole. *Emotional and Physical Pain are Almost the*
Same to Your Brain. www.forbes.com/sites/nicolefisher/
2020/02/14/emotional--physical-pain-are-almost-the-\
same to-your-brain/#4abe490346c1

. . .

His Holiness the 16th Karmapa, Karma Triyana
    DharmaChakra, May 2017 Kagyu.org/the-16th-karmapa

His Holiness 17th Karmapa, *His Holiness Teachers
    Meditations for the West*, April 6,
    www.nalandabodhi.org/2015/04/06/karmapa

Iacoboni, M. *Mirroring People.* Farrar, Straus and Giroux,
    2008.

Jonas, Wayne B. "The Myth of the Placebo Response." *Frontiers in Psychiatry*, 16 August 2019,
    www.frontiersin.org/articles/10.3389/fpsyt.2019.00577.

Lama Palden Drolma. "How to Practice Dedicating Merit."09
    April   2018,   www.lionsroar.com/how-to-practice-
dedicating-merit

Lloyd, Robin. "Strange Experiments Create Body-Swapping
    Experiences." *Live Science*, 02 December, 2008. www.
livescience.com/5207-strange-experiments-create-body-
swapping-experiences.html

Marchant, Jo. *Cure, A Journey into the Science of Mind
    Over Matter,* Penguin Random House, 2016.

. . .

McGilchrist, I. *The Master and His Emissary.* Yale
University Press, 2009.

Medicine   Buddha   Mantra,   www.
landofmedicinebuddha.org/about-medicine-
buddha/meaning-of-mantra-and-praise